PENGUIN BOOKS — GREAT IDEAS

How to Achieve True Greatness

Baldesar Castiglione

1478–1529

Baldesar Castiglione

How to Achieve True Greatness

TRANSLATED BY
GEORGE BULL

PENGUIN BOOKS — GREAT IDEAS

PENGUIN BOOKS

Published by the Penguin Group
Penguin Group (USA) Inc., 375 Hudson Street, New York, New York 10014, U.S.A.
Penguin Group (Canada), 90 Eglinton Avenue East, Suite 700, Toronto,
Ontario, Canada M4P 2Y3 (a division of Pearson Penguin Canada Inc.)
Penguin Books Ltd, 80 Strand, London WC2R 0RL, England
Penguin Ireland, 25 St Stephen's Green, Dublin 2, Ireland (a division of Penguin Books Ltd)
Penguin Group (Australia), 250 Camberwell Road, Camberwell,
Victoria 3124, Australia (a division of Pearson Australia Group Pty Ltd)
Penguin Books India Pvt Ltd, 11 Community Centre, Panchsheel Park, New Delhi–110 017, India
Penguin Group (NZ), cnr Airborne and Rosedale Roads, Albany,
Auckland 1310, New Zealand (a division of Pearson New Zealand Ltd)
Penguin Books (South Africa) (Pty) Ltd, 24 Sturdee Avenue,
Rosebank, Johannesburg 2196, South Africa

Penguin Books Ltd, Registered Offices:
80 Strand, London WC2R 0RL, England

This edition published in Penguin Books (UK) 2005
Published in Penguin Books (USA) 2006

Translation copyright © George Bull, 1967
All rights reserved

Reprinted from *The Book of the Courtier*,
translated and edited by George Bull (Penguin Classics, 1967).

ISBN 0 14 30.3755 2

Printed in the United States of America

Contents

The First Book of the Courtier

I have spent a long time wondering, my dear Alfonso, which of two things was the more difficult for me: either to refuse what you have asked me so often and so insistently, or to do it. On the one hand, it seemed to me to be very hard to refuse anything, and especially something praiseworthy, to one whom I love dearly and by whom I feel I am very dearly loved; yet on the other hand, to embark on a project which I was uncertain of being able to finish seemed wrong to one who respects adverse criticism as much as it ought to be respected. Eventually, after a great deal of thought, I have made up my mind to find out how diligent I can be when helped by affection and the anxiety to please, which usually act as a sharp spur to all kinds of activity.

Now your request is that I should describe what, in my view, is the form of courtiership most appropriate for a gentleman living at the Courts of princes, by which he will have the knowledge and the ability to serve them in every reasonable thing, winning their favour and the praise of others. In short, you want to know what kind of man must be one who deserves the name of a perfect courtier and has no shortcomings whatsoever. Considering this request, I must say that, if I did not think it a greater fault to be judged wanting in love by you than wanting in prudence by others, I would have rejected the task, for fear of being accused of rashness by all those who know how difficult an undertaking it is to select from all the many and various customs followed at the Courts of Christendom the most perfect model and, as it were, the very flower of courtiership. For familiarity often causes the same things to be liked and disliked: and thus it sometimes happens that the customs, behaviour, ceremonies and ways of life approved of at one period of time grow to be looked down on, and those which were once looked down on come to be approved. So we can see clearly enough that usage is more effective than reason in introducing new things among us and in wiping out the old. And anyone who tries to judge what is perfect in these matters often deceives himself. Being well aware of this, therefore, and of the many other problems connected with the subject proposed to me, I am compelled to say something by way of excuse and to testify that what I am doing wrong (if it can be called so) you are responsible for as well, and that if I am to be blamed for it you must share the blame. After all, you must be judged to be as much at fault in imposing on me a task greater than my resources as I am in having accepted it.

But let us now begin to discuss the subject we have chosen and, if it is possible, create a courtier so perfect that the prince who is worthy of his service, even though his dominion is small, can count himself a truly great ruler. In these books we shall not follow any strict order or list a series of precepts, as is the normal practice in teaching. Instead, following many writers of the ancient world, and reviving a pleasant memory, we shall recount some discussions which once took place among men who were singularly qualified in these matters. Even though I did not take part in them in person (being in England when they were held), they were faithfully reported to me soon after my return by someone who was present, and I shall endeavour to reproduce them as accurately as my memory allows so that you may discover what was held and thought on the subject by eminent men whose judgement can always be trusted completely. Nor will it be beside the purpose, in order to continue the story in logical order, to describe the occasion of the discussions that took place.

On the slopes of the Apennines, almost in the centre of Italy towards the Adriatic, is situated, as everyone knows, the little city of Urbino. Although it is surrounded by hills which are perhaps not as agreeable as those found in many other places, none the less it has been favoured by Nature with a very rich and fertile countryside, so that as well as a salubrious atmosphere it enjoys an abundance of all the necessities of life. Among the blessings and advantages that can be claimed for it, I believe the greatest is that for a long time now it has been governed by outstanding rulers, even though in the turmoils into which Italy was plunged by war it was for a time deprived of them. Without looking any further, we can find a splendid example in Duke Federico of glorious memory, who in his day was the light of Italy. Nor are there lacking today any number of reliable witnesses to his prudence, humanity, justice, generosity and unconquerable spirit, and to his military skill, which was brilliantly attested by his many victories, his ability to capture impregnable places, his swift and decisive expeditions, his having routed many times with few troops great and formidable armies, and his never having lost a single battle. So we can fairly compare him with many famous men of the ancient world. Among his other commendable enterprises, Duke Federico built on the rugged site of Urbino a palace which many believe to be the most beautiful in all Italy; and he furnished it so well and appropriately that it seemed more like a city than a mere palace. For he adorned it not only with the usual objects, such as silver vases, wall-hangings of the richest cloth of gold, silk and other similar material, but also with countless antique statues of marble and bronze, with rare pictures, and with every kind of musical instrument; nor would he tolerate anything that was not most rare and outstanding. Then, at great cost, he collected a large number of the finest and rarest books, in Greek, Latin and Hebrew, all of which he adorned with gold and silver, believing that they were the crowning glory of his great palace.

Following, therefore, the course of Nature, and being already sixty-five years old, Duke Federico died as gloriously as he had lived, leaving as his heir his only son, a little, motherless boy of ten named Guidobaldo. And Guidobaldo seemed to inherit not only his father's state but all his virtues as well, immediately showing in his marvellous disposition the promise of more than can be expected from a mortal man. In consequence, it was widely said that of all the wonderful things that Duke

Federico had done, the greatest was to have fathered such a son. But envious of his great qualities, Fortune set herself with all her might to frustrate what had begun so nobly, with the result that before he was yet twenty years old Duke Guido fell sick with the gout which, inflicting terrible pain, grew steadily worse and within a short space of time crippled him so badly that he could neither stand nor walk. Thus one of the best and most handsome men in the whole world was deformed and ruined while still of tender age. Not satisfied even with this, Fortune so opposed him in all his projects that he rarely succeeded in what he undertook; and although he was a man of mature deliberation and unconquerable spirit, everything he set his hand to, whether in arms or anything else, great or small, always ended unhappily, as we can see from the many diverse calamities which befell him, and which he always bore with such fortitude that his will was never crushed by fate. On the contrary, with great resilience and spirit, he despised the blows of Fortune, living the life of a healthy and happy man, despite sickness and adversity, and achieving true dignity and universal renown. Thus even though he was infirm, he campaigned with a most honourable rank in the service of their Serene Highnesses Kings Alfonso and Ferdinand the Younger of Naples, and subsequently with Pope Alexander VI as well as the Signories of Venice and Florence. Then, after the accession of Pope Julius II, he was made Captain of the Church; and during this time, following his customary style of life, he saw to it that his household was filled with very noble and worthy gentlemen, with whom he lived on the most familiar terms, delighting in their company. In this the pleasure he caused others was no less than what he received, for he was very well versed in both Latin and Greek, and possessed as well as an affable and charming nature, an infinite range of knowledge. Moreover, his indomitable spirit so spurred him on that, even though he himself was unable to take part in chivalrous activities, as he once used to, he loved to see them pursued by others, and he would show his fine judgement when commenting on what they did, correcting or praising each one according to his merits. So in jousts and tournaments, in riding, in handling every kind of weapon, as well as in the festivities, games and musical performances, in short, in all the activities appropriate to a well-born gentleman, everyone at his Court strove to behave in such a way as to deserve to be judged worthy of the Duke's noble company.

So all day and every day at the Court of Urbino was spent on honourable and pleasing activities both of the body and the mind. But since the Duke always retired to his bedroom soon after supper, because of his infirmity, as a rule at that hour everyone went to join the Duchess, Elisabetta Gonzaga, with whom was always to be found signora Emilia Pia, a lady gifted with such a lively wit and judgement, as you know, that she seemed to be in command of all and to endow everyone else with her own discernment and goodness. In their company polite conversations and innocent pleasantries were heard, and everyone's face was so full of laughter and gaiety that the house could truly be called the very inn of happiness. And I am sure that the delight and enjoyment to be had from loving and devoted companionship were never experienced elsewhere as they once were in Urbino. For, apart from the honour it was for each of us to be in the service of a ruler such as I described above, we all felt supremely happy whenever we came into the presence of the Duchess; and this sense of contentment formed between us a bond of affection so strong that even between brothers there could never have been such harmonious agreement and heartfelt love as there was among us all. It was the same with the ladies, whose company we all enjoyed very freely and innocently, since everyone was allowed to talk and sit, make jokes and laugh with whom he pleased, though such was the respect we had for the wishes of the Duchess that the liberty we enjoyed was accompanied by the most careful restraint. And without exception everyone considered that the most pleasurable thing possible was to please her and the most displeasing thing in the world was to earn her displeasure. So for these reasons in her company the most decorous behaviour proved compatible with the greatest freedom, and in her presence our games and laughter were seasoned both with the sharpest witticisms and with a gracious and sober dignity. For the modesty and nobility which informed every act, word and gesture of the Duchess, in jest and laughter, caused even those seeing her for the first time to recognize that she was a very great lady. It seemed, from the way in which she influenced those around her, that she tempered us all to her own character and quality, so that everyone endeavoured to imitate her personal way of behaviour, deriving as it were a model of fine manners from the presence of so great and talented a woman, whose high qualities I do not intend to describe now, since this is not to my purpose and they are well known to all the world, apart from being beyond the reach of whatever I could say or write. But I must add that those qualities in the Duchess which might have remained somewhat hidden, Fortune, as if admiring such rare virtues, chose to reveal through many adversities and harsh blows, in order to demonstrate that in the tender soul of a woman, and accompanied by singular beauty, there may also dwell prudence and a courageous spirit and all those virtues very rarely found even in the staunchest of men.

To continue, let me say that it was the custom for all the gentlemen of the house to go, immediately after supper, to the rooms of the Duchess; and there, along with pleasant recreations and enjoyments of various kinds, including constant music and dancing, sometimes intriguing questions were asked, and sometimes ingenious games played (now on the suggestion of one person and now of another) in which, using various ways of concealment, those present revealed their thoughts in allegories to this person or that. And occasionally, there would be discussions on various subjects, or there would be a sharp exchange of spontaneous witticisms; and often 'emblems', as we call them nowadays, were devised for the occasion. And everyone enjoyed these exchanges immensely, since, as I have said, the house was full of very noble and talented persons.

[. . .]

The rule was that as soon as anyone came into the presence of the Duchess he would take his place in a circle, sitting down wherever he wished or wherever he happened to find himself; the group was arranged alternately one man and one woman, as long as there were women, for invariably they were outnumbered by the men. Then the company was governed according to the wishes of the Duchess, who usually left this task to signora Emilia. So the day after the Pope's departure, they all assembled in the customary place at the usual time, and after many pleasant discussions, the Duchess decided that signora Emilia should begin the games.

[. . .]

Everyone was waiting for signora Emilia when without saying a word to Bembo she turned to Federico Fregoso and indicated that he should say what game he would suggest; and he immediately began as follows:

'Madam, [. . .] To teach a lesson to the many fools who in their presumption and absurdity think they are entitled to be called good courtiers, I would like our game this evening to be this: that one of us should be chosen and given the task of depicting in words a perfect courtier, explaining the character and the particular qualities needed by anyone who deserves such a title. And, just as in philosophical disputations, if anything is said which does not seem appropriate, each of us may be allowed to contradict.'

Federico was continuing to speak, when signora Emilia interrupted him to say: 'If the Duchess wishes, this will be our game for this evening.'

And the Duchess answered: 'Yes, that is my wish.'

Then almost without exception all those who were present began to say among themselves and to the Duchess that this was the best game of all; and hardly waiting to hear each other talk, they all urged signora Emilia to decide who should make a start. So, turning to the Duchess, she said:

'Decide, madam, who it is you wish to undertake this task; for I don't want in choosing one rather than another to appear to be judging whom I think the most capable, and so give offence.'

The Duchess answered: 'No, you must make the choice yourself; and take care lest by disobeying me you set a bad example to the others to do the same.'

Then, with a smile, signora Emilia said to Count Lodovico da Canossa:

'Well, then, so that we won't lose any more time, you will be the one to undertake the task as described by Federico. Not, let me say, that we believe you are such a fine courtier that you know what befits one, but because if you say everything contrariwise, as we hope you will, then the game will be still better since everyone will have a reason for challenging you, whereas if the task were given to someone knowing more than you do, no one could contradict anything he said, since it would be the truth, and so the game would prove very dull.'

The Count immediately retorted:

'But, madam, since you are present we need have no fear that the truth would go unchallenged.

[. . .]

'Let me start by saying that to recognize true perfection in anything is so difficult as to be scarcely possible; and this because of the way opinions vary. Thus there are many who like to hear someone talking a great deal and who will call him an agreeable companion. Some will prefer reticence; others an active and restless man; others one who always acts with calmness and deliberation; and so everyone praises or condemns according to his own opinion, always camouflaging a vice under the name of the corresponding virtue, or a virtue under the name of the corresponding vice. For example, a presumptuous man will be called frank, a modest man, dull; a simple-minded man, good; a rascal, shrewd; and so on and so forth. Still, I do think there is a perfection for everything, even though it may be concealed, and I also think that this perfection can be determined through informed and reasoned argument. And since, as I have said, the truth is often concealed and I do not claim to be informed, I can only praise courtiers of the kind I esteem myself and approve what seems to my limited judgement to be nearest to what is correct; and you can follow my judgement if it seems good, or keep to your own if it differs. Nor shall I argue that mine is better than yours, for not only can you think one thing and I another but I myself can think one thing at one time and something else another time.'

*

The Count then continued: 'So, for myself, I would have our courtier of noble birth and good family, since it matters far less to a common man if he fails to perform virtuously and well than to a nobleman. For if a gentleman strays from the path of his forbears, he dishonours his family name and not only fails to achieve anything but loses what has already been achieved. Noble birth is like a bright lamp that makes clear and visible both good deeds and bad, and inspires and incites to high performance as much as fear of dishonour or hope of praise; and since their deeds do not possess such noble brilliance, ordinary people lack both this stimulus and the fear of dishonour; nor do they believe that they are bound to surpass what was achieved by their forbears. Whereas to people of noble birth it seems reprehensible not to attain at least the standard set them by their ancestors. Thus as a general rule, both in arms and in other worthy activities, those who are most distinguished are of noble birth, because Nature has implanted in everything a hidden seed which has a certain way of influencing and passing on its own essential characteristics to all that grows from it, making it similar to itself. We see this not only in breeds of horses and other animals but also in trees, whose offshoots nearly always resemble the trunk; and if they sometimes degenerate, the fault lies with the man who tends them. So it happens with men, who, if they are well tended and properly brought up, nearly always resemble those from whom they spring, and are often even better; but if they have no one to give them proper attention, they grow wild and never reach maturity. It is true that, through the favour of the stars or of Nature, certain people come into the world endowed with such gifts that they seem not to have been born but to have been formed by some god with his own hands and blessed with every possible advantage of mind and body. Similarly, there are many to be found so uncouth and absurd that it can be believed simply that Nature was motivated by spite or mockery in bringing them into the world at all. Just as even with unceasing diligence and careful training the latter cannot usually be made to bear fruit, so with only the slightest effort the former reach the summit of excellence. And to give you an example, look at Don Ippolito d'Este, Cardinal of Ferrara, whose fortunate birth has influenced his person, his appearance, his words and all his actions. Because of this favour, despite his youth, even among the most venerable cardinals he carries such weighty authority that he seems more suited to teach than to be taught. Similarly, when conversing with men and women of every sort, when playing or laughing or joking, he has such charming ways and such a gracious manner that anyone who speaks to, or merely sets eyes on the Cardinal feels a lasting affection for him. However, to return to the subject, I say that between such supreme grace and such absurd folly can be found a middle way, and that those who are not perfectly endowed by Nature can, through care and effort, polish and to a great extent correct their natural defects. So in addition to noble birth, I would have the courtier favoured in this respect, too, and receive from Nature not only talent and beauty of countenance and person but also that certain air and grace that makes him immediately pleasing and attractive to all who meet him; and this grace should be an adornment informing and accompanying all his actions, so that he appears clearly worthy of the companionship and favour of the great.'

Then, refusing to wait any longer, signor Gaspare Pallavicino remarked:

'So that our game may proceed as it is meant to, and to show that we are not forgetting our privilege of contradicting, let me say that I do not believe that nobility of birth is necessary for the courtier. And if I thought I was saying something new to us, I would cite many people who, though of the most noble blood, have been wicked in the extreme, and, on the other hand, many of humble birth who, through their virtues, have won glory for their descendants. And if what you have just said is true, namely, that concealed in everything is the influence of its first seed, we should all be of the same character, since we all had the same beginning; nor would anyone be more noble than another. In fact, I hold that the various gradations of elevation and lowliness that exist among us have many other causes. The first and foremost is Fortune, who rules everything that happens in this world, and often appears to amuse herself by exalting whomever she pleases, regardless of merit, or hurling down those worthiest of being raised up. I fully concur with what you said about the happiness of those endowed at birth with all the perfections of mind and body; but this is seen among those of humble origins as well as those of noble birth, since Nature has no regard for these fine distinctions. On the contrary, as I have said, the finest gifts of Nature are often found in persons of very humble family. Therefore, since this nobility of birth is acquired neither through talent nor through force or skill, and is a matter for congratulating one's ancestors rather than oneself, it seems very odd to insist that, if the courtier's parents are of low birth, all his good qualities are spoilt and the other qualities you have mentioned are insufficient to bring him to the height of perfection: these being talent, good looks and disposition, and the grace which makes a person always pleasing at first sight.'

Count Lodovico answered: 'I do not deny that the same virtues can exist in men of low birth as in those of noble family. However, not to repeat what we have said already, let me give one more reason among many for praising nobility of birth, which, since it stands to reason that good should beget good, everyone always respects; and it is that (since we are to create a courtier without any defects, and endowed with every kind of merit) he must be a nobleman if only because of the immediate impression this makes on all concerned. For given two gentlemen of the Court, neither of whom as yet has shown what he is like by his actions, either good or bad, as soon as it is discovered that one of them was well born and the other not, the latter will be respected far less than the former, and only after a great deal of time and effort will he win the good opinion that the other acquires instantly, merely because of his nobility. It is well understood how important these impressions are, for, speaking of ourselves, we have seen men coming to this house who, although very stupid and dull, have been regarded throughout Italy as very great courtiers; and even though they were eventually found out, they still fooled us for a long time and sustained in our minds the opinion of themselves already formed before they arrived, despite the fact that their behaviour was in keeping with their lack of merit. We have seen others, who were regarded with very little favour to begin with, eventually meet with great success. Now there are various reasons for these mistakes, including the obstinacy of princes who, in the hope of achieving a miraculous transformation, sometimes deliberately favour someone who they know does not deserve it. Then again, sometimes they are themselves deceived; but, since princes always have countless imitators, their favour confers considerable fame which in turn influences the rest of us. And if people discover something that seems to contradict the prevailing opinion, they accept that they are mistaken and they always wait for some revelation. This is because it seems that what is universally believed must be based on true and reasonable grounds. Moreover, we are always most anxious to take sides either passionately for or against, as can be seen in public combats or games or any kind of contest, where the onlookers often for no clear reason favour one or other of the participants, desperately anxious that he should win and his opponent lose. Then as regards men's characters, their good or bad reputation, as soon as we hear of it, arouses in us either love or hatred, so that for the most part we judge on the basis of one of these emotions. So you see how important are first impressions, and how hard a man must strive to give a good impression at the beginning if he is ambitious to win the rank and name of a good courtier.

'But to come to specific details, I judge that the first and true profession of the courtier must be that of arms; and this above everything else I wish him to pursue vigorously. Let him also stand out from the rest as enterprising, bold, and loyal to whomever he serves. And he will win a good reputation by demonstrating these qualities whenever and wherever possible, since failure to do so always incurs the gravest censure. Just as once a woman's reputation for purity has been sullied it can never be restored, so once the reputation of a gentleman-at-arms has been stained through cowardice or some other reproachful behaviour, even if only once, it always remains defiled in the eyes of the world and covered with ignominy. The more our courtier excels in this art, therefore, the more praise he will deserve, although I do not think he needs to have the professional knowledge of such things and the other qualities appropriate to a military commander. However, since the subject of what constitutes a great captain takes us into very deep waters, we shall be content, as we said, for the courtier to show complete loyalty and an undaunted spirit, and for these to be always in evidence. For men demonstrate their courage far more often in little things than in great. Very often in the face of appalling danger but where there are numerous witnesses one will find those who, though ready to drop dead with fear, driven on by shame or the presence of others, will press forward, with their eyes closed, and do their duty; and only God knows how. But in things of trifling importance, when they believe they can avoid danger without its being noticed, they are only too willing to play for safety. As for those who, even when they are sure they are not being observed or seen or recognized by anyone, are full of ardour and avoid doing anything, no matter how trivial, for which they would incur reproach, they possess the temper and quality we are looking for in our courtier. All the same, we do not wish the courtier to make a show of being so fierce that he is always blustering and bragging, declaring that he is married to his cuirass, and glowering with the haughty looks that we know only too well in Berto. To these may very fairly be said what a worthy lady once remarked jokingly, in polite company, to a certain man (I don't want just now to mention him by name) whom she had honoured by asking him to dance and who not only refused but would not listen to music or take part in the many other entertainments offered, protesting all the while that such frivolities were not his business. And when at length the lady asked what his business was, he answered with a scowl: "Fighting . . ."

'"Well then," the lady retorted, "I should think that since you aren't at war at the moment and you are not engaged in fighting, it would be a good thing if you were to have yourself well greased and stowed away in a cupboard with all your fighting equipment, so that you avoid getting rustier than you are already."

'And of course everyone burst out laughing at the way she showed her contempt for his stupid presumption.

'Therefore,' Count Lodovico went on, 'the man we are seeking should be fierce, rough and always to the fore, in the presence of the enemy; but anywhere else he should be kind, modest, reticent and anxious above all to avoid ostentation or the kind of outrageous self-glorification by which a man always arouses loathing and disgust among those who have to listen to him.'

'As for me,' signor Gaspare replied, 'I have very seldom known men who are any good at anything who do not praise themselves. It seems to me that it is only right to allow them to do so, since, when a man who knows he is of some worth sees what he does being ignored, he grows angry at the way his qualities are hidden from sight and is forced to reveal them in some way lest he be cheated of the honour which is the rightful prize for virtuous endeavour. Thus, among the writers of the ancient world, rarely does anyone of any worth refrain from praising himself. Those who praise themselves even though they lack merit are certainly intolerable; but then we assume that our courtier will not be one of them.'

At this, the Count said:

'If you were listening, what I did was to censure those who praise themselves extravagantly and brashly. But I certainly agree that it would be wrong to take exception when a worthy man indulges in some modest self-praise; indeed it is then more convincing than if it comes from someone else. What I am saying is that a man who praises himself in the right way, and does not cause envy or annoyance in doing so, is well within the bounds of discretion; and he deserves the praise of others as well as what he allows himself, because he is achieving something very difficult.'

'You must teach us how to do it,' remarked signor Gaspare.

'Well,' the Count replied, 'there are those who taught this among the writers of the ancient world. However, in my opinion it all depends on saying things in such a way that they do not seem to be spoken with that end in view, but are so very much to the purpose that one cannot refrain from saying them; and also on giving the impression of avoiding self-praise, while indulging in it: but not in the style of those braggarts who open their mouths and let the words pour out heedlessly. As one of our own did the other day, who, after he had had his thigh run through by a spear at Pisa, said he thought a fly had stung him; and another who said he didn't keep a looking-glass in his room because when he lost his temper his expression was so terrible that if he saw it he would frighten himself to death.'

Everyone laughed at this, but Cesare Gonzaga added:

'What are you laughing at? Don't you know that after Alexander the Great had heard that in the opinion of a certain philosopher there were countless other worlds, he began to weep, and when asked why he did so, he replied: "Because I haven't yet conquered a single one" – as if he had it in him to conquer them all? Doesn't this seem to you to be more boastful than that remark about the fly?'

Then the Count remarked:

'And Alexander was a greater man than the one who

mentioned the fly. But surely we must forgive outstanding men when they presume too much of themselves? After all, a man who has to achieve great things must have the courage to do them and must have confidence in himself. He should not be cowardly or abject, though he should be modest in his words, presuming less of himself than he achieves and being careful, too, that his presumption does not turn to rashness.'

After the Count had fallen silent for a moment, Bernardo Bibbiena said, with a smile:

'I remember your saying earlier that this courtier of ours should be naturally endowed with beauty of countenance and person and with an attractive grace. Well, I feel sure that I possess both grace and beauty of countenance, and that's why so many women, as you know, are madly in love with me. But when it comes to the beauty of my person, I am rather doubtful, and especially as regards these legs of mine which do not seem to me to be as good as I would wish; still, as to my chest and so on, I am quite satisfied. So please explain in more detail about what shape of body one should have, so that I can extricate myself from doubt and put my mind at rest.'

After everyone had laughed at this for a moment, the Count said:

'Certainly it's no lie to say that you possess the grace of countenance that I mentioned, and I have no need of any other example to illustrate it; for undoubtedly we can see that your appearance is very agreeable and pleasing to all, even if your features are not very delicate, though then again you manage to appear both manly and grace-ful. This is a quality found in many different kinds of faces. And I would like our courtier to have the same aspect. I don't want him to appear soft and feminine as so many try to do, when they not only curl their hair and pluck their eyebrows but also preen themselves like the most wanton and dissolute creatures imaginable. Indeed, they appear so effeminate and languid in the way they walk, or stand, or do anything at all, that their limbs look as if they are about to fall apart; and they pronounce their words in such a drawling way that it seems as if they are about to expire on the spot. And the more they find themselves in the company of men of rank, the more they carry on like that. Since Nature has not in fact made them the ladies they want to seem and be, they should be treated not as honest women but as common whores and be driven out from all gentlemanly society, let alone the Courts of great lords.

'Then, as for the physical appearance of the courtier, I would say that all that is necessary is that he should be neither too small nor too big, since either of these two conditions causes a certain contemptuous wonder and men built in this way are stared at as if they were monsters. However, if one is forced to choose between the two evils, then it is better to be on the small side than unduly large; for men who are so huge are often found to be rather thick-headed, and moreover, they are also unsuited for sport and recreation, which I think most important for the courtier. So I wish our courtier to be well built, with finely proportioned members, and

I would have him demonstrate strength and lightness and suppleness and be good at all the physical exercises befitting a warrior. Here, I believe, his first duty is to know how to handle expertly every kind of weapon, either on foot or mounted, to understand all their finer points, and to be especially well informed about all those weapons commonly used among gentlemen. For apart from their use in war, when perhaps the finer points may be neglected, often differences arise between one gentleman and another and lead to duels, and very often the weapons used are those that come immediately to hand. So, for safety's sake, it is important to know about them. And I am not one of those who assert that all skill is forgotten in a fight; because anyone who loses his skill at such a time shows that he has allowed his fear to rob him of his courage and his wits.

'I also believe that it is of the highest importance to know how to wrestle, since this often accompanies combat on foot. Next, both for his own sake and for his friends, the courtier should understand about seeking restitution and the conduct of disputes, and he should be skilled in seizing the advantage, and in all this he must show both courage and prudence. Nor should he be too anxious for these engagements, save when his honour demands it; for, as well as the considerable danger that an uncertain outcome brings with it, whoever rushes into these things precipitately and without urgent cause deserves to be gravely censured, even if he is successful. However, when a man has committed himself so far that he cannot withdraw without reproach then both in the preliminaries and in the duel itself he should be very deliberate. He should always show readiness and courage; and he should not behave like those who are always quibbling and arguing over points of honour, and when they have the choice of weapons, select those which can neither cut nor prick, arm themselves as if they had to face a cannonade, and thinking it enough if they are not defeated, retreat all the time and keep on the defensive, giving proof of utter cowardice, and in this way making themselves the sport of children, like those two men from Ancona who fought at Perugia a little while ago, and made everyone who saw them burst out laughing.'

'And who were they?' asked Gaspare Pallavicino.

'Two cousins,' answered Cesare.

'And in their fighting, more like two dear brothers,' said the Count. Then he continued:

'Weapons are also often used in various sports during peacetime, and gentlemen often perform in public spectacles before the people and before ladies and great lords. So I wish our courtier to be an accomplished and versatile horseman and, as well as having a knowledge of horses and all the matters to do with riding, he should put every effort and diligence into surpassing the rest just a little in everything, so that he may always be recognized as superior. And as we read of Alcibiades, that he surpassed all those peoples among whom he lived, and each time in regard to what they claimed to be best at, so this courtier of ours should outstrip all others, and in regard to the things they know well. Thus it is the peculiar excellence of the Italians to ride well with the rein, to handle spirited horses very skilfully, and to tilt and joust;

so in all this the courtier should compare with the best of them. In tourneys, in holding his ground, in forcing his way forward, he should compare with the best of the French; in volleying, in running bulls, in casting spears and darts, he should be outstanding among the Spaniards. But, above all, he should accompany his every act with a certain grace and fine judgement if he wishes to earn that universal regard which everyone covets.

'There are also many other sports which, although they do not directly require the use of weapons, are closely related to arms and demand a great deal of manly exertion. Among these it seems to me that hunting is the most important, since in many ways it resembles warfare; moreover, it is the true pastime of great lords, it is a suitable pursuit for a courtier, and we know that it was very popular in the ancient world. It is also fitting that the courtier should know how to swim, jump, run and cast the stone for, apart from the usefulness of these accomplishments in war, one is often required to display one's skill and such sports can help to build up a good reputation, especially with the crowd which the courtier always has to humour. Another noble sport which is very suitable for the courtier to play is tennis, for this shows how well he is built physically, how quick and agile he is in every member, and whether he has all the qualities demonstrated in most other games. I think no less highly of performing on horseback, which is certainly very exhausting and difficult but more than anything else serves to make a man wonderfully agile and dextrous; and apart from its usefulness, if agility on horseback is accompanied by gracefulness, in my opinion it makes a finer spectacle than any other sport. Then if our courtier possesses more than average skill in all these sports, I think he should ignore the others, such as turning cartwheels, tight-rope walking and that kind of thing, since these are more like acrobatics and hardly suitable for a gentleman. Then again, since one cannot always be taking part in such strenuous exercises (besides which constant repetition causes satiety and destroys the regard we have for rare things) one must always be sure to give variety to the way one lives by doing different things. So I would like the courtier sometimes to descend to calmer and more restful games, and to escape envy and enter pleasantly into the company of all the others by doing everything they do; although he should never fail to behave in a commendable manner and should rule all his actions with that good judgement which will not allow him to take part in any foolishness. Let him laugh, jest, banter, romp and dance, though in a fashion that always reflects good sense and discretion, and let him say and do everything with grace.'

Then Cesare Gonzaga said: 'It is certainly too soon to interrupt this discussion, but if I stay silent I shall not be taking advantage of my privilege of speaking and I shall fail to learn something more. And I hope I may be forgiven if I ask a question instead of contradicting. I believe this may be allowed me, following the example set by our Bernardo who, through his excessive desire to be thought handsome, has already violated the laws of our game by doing the same.'

'You see,' the Duchess commented, 'how a single transgression leads to any number of others. So the one who sins and gives a bad example, as Bernardo has done, deserves to be punished not only for his wrongdoing but also for that of the others.'

Then Cesare remarked: 'In that case, madam, I will be exempt from any penalty, since Bernardo is to be punished both for his own transgression and for mine.'

'On the contrary,' said the Duchess, 'you must both of you be punished twice: he for his own wrongdoing and for having persuaded you to err, and you for your own mistake and for having imitated the criminal.'

'Madam,' answered Cesare, 'I've done nothing criminal so far; so in order to let Bernardo have all the punishment to himself I'll keep quiet.'

He had already stopped talking when signora Emilia said with a laugh:

'Say whatever you please, because, if the Duchess allows, I shall forgive both the one who has transgressed and the one who is going to do something nearly as bad.'

Said the Duchess: 'Very well, then. But take care you do not deceive yourself and perhaps think that you deserve more praise for being clement than for being just. For if one is too forgiving with a transgressor, one injures the innocent. However, I don't want my sternness in reproaching your indulgence to mean that we fail to hear what Cesare has to ask.'

So then, at a sign from the Duchess and from signora Emilia, he at once began:

★

'If I remember rightly, my dear Count, it seems to me that you have repeated several times this evening that the courtier has to imbue with grace his movements, his gestures, his way of doing things and in short, his every action. And it appears to me that you require this in everything as the seasoning without which all other attributes and good qualities would be almost worthless. Now I admit that everyone should easily be persuaded of this, seeing that, by the very meaning of the word, it can be said that a man who behaves with grace finds it with others. You have said that this is very often a natural, God-given gift, and that even if it is not quite perfect it can be greatly enhanced by application and effort. It seems to me that those who are born as fortunate and as rich in such treasures as some we know have little need of any further instruction, since the gracious favour they have received from heaven raises them, almost despite themselves, higher than they might have desired, and makes everyone both like and admire them. I do not argue about this, since it is not in our power to acquire it of ourselves. But regarding those who receive from Nature only so much as to make it possible for them to acquire grace through enterprise, application and effort, I should like to know by what art, teaching and method they can gain this grace, both in sport and recreation which you believe are so important, and in everything else they say or do. Now since by praising this quality so highly you have, I believe, aroused in all of us a strong desire to obtain it, because of the task given you by signora Emilia, you are also obliged to satisfy us by teaching the way to do so.'

★

'I am not obliged,' said the Count, 'to teach you how to acquire grace, or indeed anything else, but only to show you what a perfect courtier should be. And I would not undertake the task of teaching you how to acquire this quality, especially as a little while ago I said that the courtier ought to know how to wrestle, and vault and so many other things which, never having learned them myself, I'm sure you know full well how I could teach them. Let it be enough that just as a good soldier knows how to tell the smith what style and shape and quality his armour should be, and yet cannot teach him how to hammer or temper it, so perhaps I shall know how to tell you what a perfect courtier should be, but not be able to teach you what you have to do to become one. However, although it is almost proverbial that grace cannot be learned, to satisfy your request as far as I can, I say that if anyone is to acquire grace as a sportsman or athlete (first assuming that he is not disqualified by Nature) he should start young and learn the principles from the best teachers. How important this seemed to King Philip of Macedon, for instance, can be seen from the fact that he wanted it to be Aristotle, the eminent philosopher, and perhaps the greatest ever, who should teach the elements of letters to his son Alexander. Then, coming to our own contemporaries, consider the physical grace and agility of Signor Galleazzo Sanseverino, Grand Equerry of France, who performs so well in this respect because in addition to his natural aptitude he has made every endeavour to learn from good teachers and to keep company with outstanding men, taking from each of them the best he can give. Thus just as for wrestling, vaulting and the handling of various kinds of weapons he has taken as his guide our Pietro Monte, who as you know is the sole and unchallenged master in regard to every kind of trained strength and agility, so for riding, jousting and so forth he has always taken as his models those who have won recognition for such skills.

'Therefore anyone who wants to be a good pupil must not only do things well but must also make a constant effort to imitate and, if possible, exactly reproduce his master. And when he feels he has made some progress it is very profitable for him to observe different kinds of courtiers and, ruled by the good judgement that must always be his guide, take various qualities now from one man and now from another. Just as in the summer fields the bees wing their way among the plants from one flower to the next, so the courtier must acquire this grace from those who appear to possess it and take from each one the quality that seems most commendable. And he should certainly not act like a friend of ours, whom you all know, who thought that he greatly resembled King Ferdinand the Younger of Aragon, but had not tried to imitate him except in the way he raised his head and twisted a corner of his mouth, a habit which the King had acquired through illness. There are many like this, who think they are marvellous if they can simply resemble a great man in some one thing; and often they seize on the only defect he has. However, having already thought a great deal about how this grace is acquired, and leaving aside those who are endowed with it by their stars, I have discovered a universal rule which seems to apply more than any other in all human actions or words: namely, to steer away from affectation at all costs, as if it were a rough and dangerous reef, and (to use perhaps a novel word for it) to practise in all things a certain nonchalance which conceals all artistry and makes whatever one says or does seem uncontrived and effortless. I am sure that grace springs especially from this, since everyone knows how difficult it is to accomplish some unusual feat perfectly, and so facility in such things excites the greatest wonder; whereas, in contrast, to labour at what one is doing and, as we say, to make bones over it, shows an extreme lack of grace and causes everything whatever its worth, to be discounted. So we can truthfully say that true art is what does not seem to be art; and the most important thing is to conceal it, because if it is revealed this discredits a man completely and ruins his reputation. I remember once having read of certain outstanding orators of the ancient world who, among the other things they did, tried hard to make everyone believe that they were ignorant of letters; and, dissembling their knowledge, they made their speeches appear to have been composed very simply and according to the promptings of Nature and truth rather than effort and artifice. For if the people had known of their skills, they would have been frightened of being deceived. So you see that to reveal intense application and skill robs everything of grace. Who is there among you who doesn't laugh when our Pierpaolo dances in that way of his, with those little jumps and with his legs stretched on tiptoe, keeping his head motionless, as if he were made of wood, and all so laboured that he seems to be counting every step? Who is so blind that he doesn't see in this the clumsiness of affectation? And in contrast we see in many of the men and women who are with us now, that graceful and nonchalant spontaneity (as it is often called) because of which they seem to be paying little, if any, attention to the way they speak or laugh or hold themselves, so that those who are watching them imagine that they couldn't and wouldn't ever know how to make a mistake.'

[. . .]

At this point, signora Emilia interrupted: 'It seems to me that this argument of yours has grown too protracted and tedious. So it would be as well to postpone it to another time.'

Federico started to answer all the same, but signora Emilia refused to let him; and eventually the Count remarked:

'There are many who want to judge style and discuss the rhythms of language and the question of imitation, yet cannot explain to me what style and rhythm are, or how to define imitation, or why things taken from Homer or someone else read so well in Virgil that they seem improved rather than plagiarized. Perhaps the reason for this is that I am not capable of understanding them. But since it is a convincing proof of whether a man understands something that he has the ability to teach it, I fear that they understand it very little themselves, and that they praise both Virgil and Cicero because they are aware that many others praise them and not because they recognize the difference between them and the rest. For certainly the difference does not consist in their preserving a few words or so in a usage different from that of the others. In Sallust, in Caesar, in Varro and in other good writers we find several terms used differently from the way Cicero employs them; yet both ways are perfectly acceptable, since the strength and genius of a language does not consist in such trifles: as Demosthenes rightly said to Aeschines, who asked him sarcastically whether some of the words he had used, which were not Attic, were monsters or portents; and Demosthenes simply laughed at this and replied that the fortunes of Greece hardly depended on that. So what cause should I have to worry if some Tuscan or other reproved me for saying *satisfatto* rather than *sodisfatto*, *onorevole* rather than *orrevole*, *causa* rather than *cagione*, *populo* rather than *popolo* and so forth?'*

At this Federico stood up and exclaimed: 'Now I beg you, listen to me for a moment.'

But signora Emilia said with a laugh: 'No, I shall be most displeased with any one of you who continues with this subject at the moment, for I wish the discussion to be postponed until another evening. But you, my dear Count, please continue with your discussion of the courtier, and show us what a good memory you have, because I think that if you can begin where you left off it will be quite a feat.'

---

* The Italian words cited by Count Lodovico mean: satisfied, honourable, cause and people.

'I fear,' answered the Count, 'that I have lost the thread. However, unless I am mistaken, we were saying that the taint of affectation always robs everything of grace and that the highest degree of grace is conferred by simplicity and nonchalance, in praise of which, and in condemnation of affectation, much more could be said. However, I want to add just one more thing and that is all. Now, every woman is extremely anxious to be beautiful or at least, failing that, to appear so. So when Nature has fallen short in some way, she endeavours to remedy the failure by artificial means. That is why we have women beautifying their faces so carefully and sometimes painfully, plucking their eyebrows and forehead, and using all those tricks and suffering all those little agonies which you ladies imagine men know nothing about but which they know only too well.'

Here, madonna Costanza Fregoso laughed and said: 'It would be far more courteous of you to continue with your discussion and to say what is the source of grace and speak of courtiership, rather than seek to expose the faults of women to no purpose.'

'On the contrary, it is very much to the purpose,' answered the Count, 'because these faults of yours that I mention rob you of grace, seeing that they spring only from affectation, through which you make it clear to everyone that you are excessively anxious to be beautiful. Surely you realize how much more graceful a woman is who, if indeed she wishes to do so, paints herself so sparingly and so little that whoever looks at her is unsure whether she is made-up or not, in comparison with one whose face is so encrusted that she seems to be wearing a mask and who dare not laugh for fear of causing it to crack, and who changes colour only when she dresses in the morning, after which she stays stock-still all the rest of the day, like a wooden statue, letting herself be seen only by torchlight, in the way a wily merchant shows his cloth in a dark corner. How much more attractive than all the others is a pretty woman who is quite clearly wearing no make-up on her face, which is neither too pallid nor too red, and whose own colouring is natural and somewhat pale (but who occasionally blushes openly from embarrassment or for some other reason), who lets her unadorned hair fall casually and unarranged, and whose gestures are simple and natural, betraying no effort or anxiety to be beautiful. Such is the uncontrived simplicity which is most attractive to the eyes and minds of men, who are always afraid of being tricked by art. In a woman, lovely teeth are always very pleasing, for since they are hidden from view most of the time, unlike the rest of the face, it can be believed that less effort has been spent on making them look beautiful; and yet those who laugh to no purpose and merely to display their teeth, betray their artificiality, and however good-looking they may be would seem to everyone most ungraceful, like Catullus' Egnatius. The same is true of the hands which, if they are delicate and fine, and are uncovered at the right time, when there is need to use and not just to display their beauty, leave one with a great desire to see more of them, especially after they have been covered again with gloves. For it appears that the person who covers them hardly cares or worries whether they are seen or not, and has beautiful hands more by Nature than through any effort or design. Surely, too, you have sometimes noticed when a woman, passing along the street on her way perhaps to church, happens, in play or for some other reason, to raise just enough of her skirts to reveal her foot and often a little of her leg as well. Does it not strike you as a truly graceful sight if she is seen just at that moment, delightfully feminine, showing her velvet ribbons and pretty stockings? Certainly I find it very agreeable, as I'm sure you all do, because everyone assumes that elegance in a place where it is generally hidden from view must be uncontrived and natural rather than carefully calculated, and that it cannot be intended to win admiration.

'In this way affectation is avoided or hidden; and now you can see how incompatible it is with gracefulness and how it robs of charm every movement of the body or of the soul, about which, admittedly, we have so far said very little. However, we should not neglect it; for, as the soul is far more worthy than the body, it deserves to be all the more cultivated and adorned. As for what our courtier ought to do in this respect, we shall leave aside the precepts of all the many wise philosophers who have written on the subject, defining the virtues of the soul and discussing their worth with such subtlety; instead, keeping to our purpose, we shall state very simply that it is enough if he is, as we say, a man of honour and integrity. For this includes prudence, goodness, fortitude and temperance of soul, and all the other qualities proper to so honourable a name. And I believe that he alone is a true moral philosopher who wishes to be good; and for this he needs few precepts other than the ambition itself. Therefore Socrates was perfectly right in affirming that in his opinion his teaching bore good fruit when it encouraged someone to strive to know and understand virtue; for those who have reached the stage where they desire nothing more eagerly than to be good have no trouble in learning all that is necessary. So I shall say no more about this.

'However, in addition to goodness, I believe that for all of us the true and principal adornment of the mind is letters; although the French, I know, recognize only the nobility of arms and think nothing of all the rest; and so they not only do not appreciate learning but detest it, regarding men of letters as basely inferior and thinking it a great insult to call anyone a scholar.'

Then the Magnifico Giuliano remarked:

'You are right in saying that this error has prevailed among the French for a long time now; but if good fortune has it that Monseigneur d'Angoulême, as it is hoped, succeeds to the throne, then I believe that just as the glory of arms flourishes and shines in France, so also with the greatest brilliance must that of letters. For, when I was at that Court not so long ago, I set eyes on this prince, and it seemed to me that, besides his handsome looks, there was such an air of greatness about him, accompanied, however, by a certain gracious humanity, that the kingdom of France on its own must always seem too limited for him. And subsequently from many gentlemen, both French and Italian, I heard a great deal in praise of his noble courtesy, his magnanimity, his valour and his generous spirit; and among other things I was told that he greatly loved and esteemed learning and respected all men of letters, and that he condemned the French themselves for being so hostile to this profession, especially as they have in their midst as magnificent a university as Paris, where people flock from all over the world.'

Then the Count added: 'It is a marvellous thing that at such a tender age, guided solely by his natural instincts and departing from the usual attitudes of his countrymen, he should of himself have chosen so commendable a path. And since subjects always imitate the behaviour of their rulers, it could well be, as you say, that the French may yet come to value learning at its true worth. They could easily be persuaded to if they would listen to reason, since nothing is more naturally desired by men or more proper to them than knowledge, and it is the height of folly to say or believe that it is not always a good thing.

'If I could speak with them or with others whose opinion does not agree with mine I would endeavour to show them how useful and necessary letters are to human dignity and life. For they were surely given by God as his supreme gift to mankind. And I should not lack examples from among those many great commanders of the ancient world, in all of whom prowess at arms was accompanied by the glory of learning. For, as you know, Alexander revered Homer so highly that he always kept the *Iliad* at his bedside. And he gave the greatest attention not only to these studies but also to philosophical speculations, under the guidance of Aristotle. Taught by Socrates, Alcibiades used letters to increase and enhance his good qualities. The attention which Caesar gave to study is attested by his own inspired writings. It is said that Scipio Africanus constantly had by him the works of Xenophon, in which, under the name of Cyrus, is drawn the portrait of a perfect king. I could cite Lucullus, Sulla, Pompey, Brutus and many other Romans and Greeks; but I shall just remind you that so excellent a commander as Hannibal, though naturally fierce and a stranger to humanity, treacherous and contemptuous both of men and the gods, none the less was something of a scholar and understood the Greek language. And if I am not mistaken I once read that he even left a book written by himself in Greek. But there is no call to tell you this, since I well know that you all realize how wrong the French are in thinking that letters are detrimental to arms. You know that in war what really spurs men on to bold deeds is the desire for glory, whereas anyone who acts for gain or from any other motive not only fails to accomplish anything worth while but deserves to be called a miserable merchant rather than a gentleman. And it is true glory that is entrusted to the sacred treasury of letters, as everyone knows except those who are so unfortunate as not to have made their acquaintance. When he reads about the great deeds of Caesar, Alexander, Scipio, Hannibal and all the others, who is so cringing, timorous and abject that he does not burn with the ambition to emulate them and is not ready to relinquish his all too brief natural life in favour of an almost eternal fame, which makes him live on more splendidly after death? But those who do not appreciate the pleasures of learning cannot realize how great is the glory that they preserve for so long, and measure it only by the life of one or two men, since their own memories are limited. The kind of glory of which they have experience is nothing in comparison with the almost everlasting glory about which, unfortunately, they know nothing; and since, therefore, glory means so little to them, we may reasonably believe that, unlike those who understand its nature, they will run few risks in pursuing it. Now someone may object to what I am saying and attempt to disprove it by various examples: citing, for instance, the knowledge of letters shown by the Italians compared with their lack of valour on the battlefield during recent years. This is only too true; but surely it may be said that here the weakness of a few has inflicted grave misfortune along with lasting infamy on the many, and they are responsible for our ruin and the way our spirit has been weakened if not crushed. Yet it would be more shameful for us to make this known to the world than it is for the French to be ignorant of letters; so it is better to pass over in silence what we cannot recall without sorrow, and leaving this subject (which I took up unwillingly) to return to our courtier.

'I should like our courtier to be a more than average scholar, at least in those studies which we call the humanities; and he should have a knowledge of Greek as well as Latin, because of the many different things that are so beautifully written in that language. He should be very well acquainted with the poets, and no less with the orators and historians, and also skilled at writing both verse and prose, especially in our own language; for in addition to the satisfaction this will give him personally, it will enable him to provide constant entertainment for the ladies, who are usually very fond of such things. But if because of his other activities or through lack of study he fails to achieve a commendable standard in his writing, then he should take pains to suppress his work, to avoid ridicule, and he should show it only to a friend he can trust. And the exercise of writing will be profitable for him at least to the extent that it will teach him how to judge the work of others. For it is very unusual for someone who is not a practised writer, however erudite he may be, to understand completely the demanding work done by writers, or appreciate their stylistic accomplishments and triumphs and those subtle details characteristic of the writers of the ancient world. Moreover, these studies will make our courtier well informed and eloquent and (as Aristippus said to the tyrant) self-confident and assured no matter whom he is talking to. However, I should like our courtier to keep one precept firmly in mind: namely, that in what I have just discussed and in everything else he should always be diffident and reserved rather than forward, and he should be on his guard against assuming that he knows what he does not know. For we are instinctively all too greedy for praise, and there is no sound or song that comes sweeter to our ears; praise, like Sirens' voices, is the kind of music that causes shipwreck to the man who does not stop his ears to its deceptive harmony. Recognizing this danger, some of the philosophers of the ancient world wrote books giving advice on how a man can tell the difference between a true friend and a flatterer. Even so, we may well ask what use is this, seeing that there are so many who realize perfectly well that they are listening to flattery, and yet love the flatterer and detest the one who tells them the truth. Indeed, very often, deciding that the one who praises them is not being fulsome enough, they lend him a hand themselves and say such things that even the most outrageous flatterer feels ashamed. Let us leave these blind fools to their errors and decide that our courtier should possess such good judgement that he will not be told that black is white or presume anything of himself unless he is certain that it is true, and especially in regard to those flaws which, if you remember, when he was suggesting his game for the evening Cesare recalled we had often used to demonstrate the particular folly of this person or another. To make no mistake at all, the courtier should, on the contrary, when he knows the praises he receives are deserved, not assent to them too openly nor let them pass without some protest. Rather he should tend to disclaim them modestly, always giving the impression that arms are, as indeed they should be, his chief profession, and that all his other fine accomplishments serve merely as adornments; and this should especially be his attitude when he is in the company of soldiers, lest he behave like those who in the world of scholarship want to be taken for warriors and among warriors want to seem men of letters. In this way, as we have said, he will avoid affectation, and even his modest achievements will appear great.'

[. . .]

The Second Book of the Courtier

'To continue the arguments of these gentlemen, which I wholly confirm and approve, I maintain that among the things we call good there are some that are always good simply in themselves, such as temperance, fortitude, health and all the virtues that foster peace of mind; and there are others that are good in various respects and depending on the end to which they are directed, such as laws, liberality, riches and so forth. I consider, therefore, that the perfect courtier, as Count Lodovico and Federico have described him, can indeed be good and praiseworthy, not, however, simply in himself but in regard to the end to which he is directed. For, to be sure, if the only fruit produced by the courtier's noble birth, gracefulness, charm and skills were just himself, I should not consider it right for a man to put into acquiring the perfection of courtiership all the study and effort that are certainly necessary. On the contrary, I should claim that many of the skills that have been attributed to him, such as dancing, entertaining, singing and playing games, were vain and frivolous, and in a man of rank deserving of censure rather than praise. For these elegances of dress, devices, mottoes and other such things that belong to the world of women and romance often, despite what many may think, serve simply to make men effeminate, to corrupt the young and to lead them into dissolute ways. And the consequences are that the name of Italy is brought into disgrace and there are few who have the courage I shall not say to die, but even to take a risk. And certainly there are countless other things which would be of far greater benefit in both peace and war, given the same amount of study and effort, than this kind of sterile courtiership. But if the activities of the courtier are directed as they should be to the virtuous end I have in mind, then I for one am quite convinced not only that they are neither harmful nor vain but that they are most advantageous and deserving of infinite praise.

'In my opinion, therefore, the end of the perfect courtier (which we have so far left untouched) is, by means of the accomplishments attributed to him by these gentlemen, so to win for himself the mind and favour of the prince he serves that he can and always will tell him the truth about all he needs to know, without fear or risk of displeasing him. And, if he knows that his prince is of a mind to do something unworthy, he should be in a position to dare to oppose him, and make courteous use of the favour his good qualities have won to remove every evil intention and persuade him to return to the path of virtue. Thus if the courtier is endowed with the goodness these gentlemen have attributed to him, as well as being quick-witted and charming, prudent and scholarly and so forth, he will always have the skill to make his prince realize the honour and advantages that accrue to him and his family from justice, liberality, magnanimity, gentleness and all the other virtues befitting a ruler, and on the other hand, the infamy and loss that result from practising the vices opposed to these virtues. Therefore I consider that just as music, festivities, games and other agreeable accomplishments are, so to speak, the flower of courtiership, so its real fruit is to encourage and help his prince to be virtuous and to deter him from evil. Then we must consider that the merit of good deeds consists in two principal things: to choose a truly virtuous end for our intentions, and to know how to find convenient and suitable means for its attainment. And so it necessarily follows that a man who strives to ensure that his prince is not deceived by anyone, does not listen to flatterers or slanderers or liars, and distinguishes between good and evil, loving the one and detesting the other, aims at the best end of all.

'It seems to me also that the accomplishments these gentlemen have attributed to the courtier can be a good means of attaining the end I have in mind; and this is because of the many faults we see in our present-day rulers the greatest are ignorance and conceit. And the root of these two evils is nothing other than falsehood, which is a vice rightly detestable to God and man and more harmful to princes than any other. For princes lack most of all what they must have in the fullest measure, namely, someone to tell them the truth and remind them of what is right. For those who are hostile to the prince are not prompted by affection to perform these offices; on the contrary, they prefer to have him live wickedly and never correct his faults. And then again, they dare not criticize the prince openly for fear of being punished. Meanwhile, among the prince's friends there are few who have free access to him, and these few are wary of reproaching him for his faults as freely as they reproach ordinary people, and often in order to win grace and favour they think only of suggesting things that are agreeable and diverting, even though they may be dishonourable and wicked. In this way, from being friends they become flatterers, and to benefit from their intimacy they always speak and act in order to gratify, and they mostly proceed by telling lies that foster ignorance in the prince's mind not only of the world around but of himself. And this can be said to be the greatest and most disastrous falsehood of all, for an ignorant mind deceives itself and lies to itself.

'The result of this is that apart from never hearing the truth of anything, princes become drunk with the power they wield, and abandoned to pleasure-seeking and amusements they become so corrupted in mind that (seeing themselves always obeyed and almost adored, with so much reverence and praise and never a hint of censure or contradiction) they pass from ignorance to extreme conceit. In consequence, they never accept anyone else's advice or opinion; and, believing that it is very easy to know how to rule and that successful government requires no art or training other than brute force, they devote all their mind and attention to maintaining the power they have and they believe that true happiness consists in being able to do what one wants. Therefore there are some princes who hate reason and justice because they think these would act as a bridle to their desires, reduce them to servitude, and if followed, rob them of the pleasures and satisfactions of their rule; and they suppose that their power would be neither perfect nor complete if they were constrained to obey the call of duty and honour, since they believe that no one who obeys is a true ruler. Therefore following on these beginnings, and letting themselves be carried away by self-conceit, they grow arrogant, and with imperious countenance and stern ways, with sumptuous dress, gold and gems, and rarely letting themselves be seen in public, they think to gain authority among men and to be regarded as gods. But these princes, to my mind, are like the giant figures that were made in Rome last year on the day of the festival in Piazza d'Agone and which outwardly looked like great men and horses in a triumph but inside were stuffed with rags and straw. However, princes of this sort are worse still. For the giant figures were held upright by their own great weight, whereas, since they are badly balanced within and out of proportion in relation to their base, the downfall of these rulers is caused by their own weight, and from one error they fall into countless others. For their ignorance and their false belief that they can do no wrong, and that their power springs from their own wisdom, prompt them to use all and every means, just or not, to usurp states whenever they have the chance.

'But if they decided to know and follow what they ought to do, then they would strive to rule in quite other ways than they do now; for they would realize how outrageous and pernicious it is when subjects, who must be governed, are wiser than the rulers who must govern them. You will agree that there is no harm in not knowing how to play music, or dance, or ride; nevertheless, a man who is not a musician is ashamed and does not dare to sing in the presence of others, or dance if he doesn't know how, or ride if he cannot sit his horse well. Yet ignorance of how to govern peoples gives rise to so many evils, so much death, destruction, burning and ruination, that it may be said to be the deadliest plague of all; and despite that some rulers who know absolutely nothing about government are not ashamed to set about the task of governing before the eyes not of a small group of men but rather of the entire world, seeing that they are so exalted in rank that all eyes are turned towards them and hence not only their great but even their slightest defects are always observed.

[. . .]

'I maintain, therefore, that since nowadays rulers are so corrupted by evil living, by ignorance and by false conceit, and it is so difficult to give them an insight into the truth and lead them to virtue, and since men seek to win their favour through lies and flattery and other wicked means, the courtier easily can and should seek to gain the goodwill of his prince by means of the noble qualities given to him by Count Lodovico and Federico. Through these, he should so win over the mind of his prince that he may go to him freely whenever he wishes to discuss any subject without hindrance. And, if he is as has been described, he will succeed in this purpose without great effort and thus he will always be able to reveal the true facts on any subject very promptly. Moreover, he will gradually be able to instil virtue into his mind, to teach him continence, fortitude, justice and temperance, and enable him to relish the sweet fruit which lies under the slight bitterness first tasted by one who is struggling against his vices, which are always as harmful, offensive and notorious as the virtues are beneficial, agreeable and universally praised. And he will be able to incite his prince to virtue by the example of those famous captains and other outstanding men of whom it was customary in the ancient world to make statues of bronze and marble, and sometimes of gold, and to erect them in public places, both to honour the great and to inspire others to work to achieve the same glory through worthy emulation.

'In this way, the courtier will be able to lead his prince along the stern path of virtue, adorning it, however, with shady fronds and strewing it with gay flowers to lessen the tedium of an arduous journey for one whose endurance is slight; and so now with music, now with arms and horses, at other times with verse or with conversations about love, and with all the means these gentlemen have suggested, he will be able to keep the prince continually absorbed in innocent pleasures, while also, as I have said, always accompanying these beguilements with emphasis on some virtuous habit, and in that way practising a healthy deception like a shrewd doctor who often spreads some sweet liquid on the rim of a cup when he wants a frail and sickly child to take a bitter medicine. Thus, under the cloak of pleasure, no matter what the time, or place, or pursuit, the courtier will always achieve his objective, and for this he will deserve far greater praise and reward than for any other good work he could possibly do. For there is nothing so advantageous to mankind as a good prince, and nothing so harmful as an evil one; and it follows that no matter how cruel and atrocious, no punishment can be enough for those courtiers who turn gentle and charming manners and noble qualities to evil ends, and by these means seek to ingratiate themselves with their prince in order to corrupt him and make him stray from the path of virtue into vice. For of these it can be said that they contaminate with deadly poison not a single cup used by one person but the public fountain at which everyone must drink.'

Signor Ottaviano fell silent, as if he were unwilling to add to what he had said. But then signor Gaspare remarked:

'It does not seem to me, signor Ottaviano, that this goodness of mind and the continence and other virtues in which you wish the courtier to instruct his lord can be learned; rather, I think that the men who possess them have been given them by Nature and by God. This must be so, since you will find that there is no one in the world so wicked and ill-disposed, or so intemperate and unjust, as to confess that he is such when he is asked; on the contrary, everyone, no matter how evil, likes to be thought just, continent and good; and this would not be the case if these virtues could be learned, for it is no disgrace not to know what one hasn't studied but

certainly shameful to lack what Nature should have
bestowed. Thus everyone tries hard to conceal his
natural defects of mind or body, as we see in the case
of the blind, the lame, the crippled and all those who
are maimed or ugly. For although these defects can be
imputed to Nature, yet no one likes to think he has
them, since then it seems that Nature herself has caused
them deliberately as a seal and token of wickedness. My
opinion in this is also confirmed by the story told of
Epimetheus, who knew so little how to distribute the
gifts of Nature among men that he left them far less well
endowed than all other creatures; and so Prometheus
stole from Minerva and Vulcan the ingenuity and knowledge by which men gain their livelihood. But they still
lacked knowledge of the civic virtues and the moral law,
because this was guarded in Jove's fortress of Olympus
by most alert guardians, by whom Prometheus was so
greatly intimidated that he dared not go near them. So
Jove, taking pity on the wretchedness of mankind (which
because of its lack of civic virtue was defenceless against
the attacks of wild beasts) sent Mercury down to earth
bearing justice and self-respect to adorn their cities and
unite the citizens. And he decided that these should not
be distributed in the same way as the other gifts of
mankind, where only one man among many needs to
be skilled (as in the case of medicine) but should be
instilled into every single person. And under the law he
ordained all those who were unjust and shameless should
be exterminated and put to death as public menaces. So
you see then, signor Ottaviano, that these virtues are

granted to men by God, and cannot be learned since they come from Nature.'

Then signor Ottaviano replied with a smile:

'So you would have it, signor Gaspare, that men are so unhappy and perverse in their judgement that they have applied themselves to discovering ways in which to tame the natures of wild beasts, bears, wolves and lions, and by the same skills can teach a pretty bird to fly where they choose it to go and return of its own will from the woods and its natural freedom to cages and captivity, and yet no matter how hard they apply themselves they cannot and will not discover ways by which to benefit themselves and improve their minds by diligence and study? In my opinion this would be as if our doctors were to study with all diligence to acquire solely the skill to heal sore nails and baby-rash and neglect treating fevers, pleurisy and other serious diseases; and as we all realize that would be quite preposterous. I consider, therefore, that the moral virtues do not come to us entirely from Nature, because nothing can ever grow accustomed to what is naturally its opposite, as we see in the case of a stone which, if it were thrown up in the air ten thousand times would still never grow accustomed to flying upwards of itself. So if the virtues were as natural to us as weight is to a stone, we would never become accustomed to vice. Nor are the vices natural to us in this way, for then we could never be virtuous; and it would be too wicked and foolish to punish men for defects that proceed from Nature through no fault of our own. This would be an error on the part of the laws, which do not inflict punishment on wrongdoers for what they have done in the past (for what is done cannot be undone) but have regard for the future, so that the one who has erred may err no more, nor cause others to do so through his bad example. So we see that the laws accept that the virtues can be learned, and this is certainly true; for we are born capable of acquiring virtues, and similarly vices, and therefore we become habituated to the one or the other through the behaviour we adopt, first of all practising the virtues or the vices, and then becoming virtuous or vicious. But the opposite is the case with qualities that are given us by Nature, which we first of all have the potentiality to practise, and then we actually practise, as in the case of the senses. For first we have the capacity to see and hear and touch and then we do see and hear and touch; although many of these faculties too are enhanced by education. For this reason, good masters not only teach children their letters but also polite manners and correct bearing in eating, drinking, speaking and walking.

'Therefore, as with other arts and skills so also with the virtues, it is necessary to have a master who by his teaching and precepts stirs and awakens the moral virtues whose seed is enclosed and buried in our souls and who, like a good farmer, cultivates and clears the way for them by removing the thorns and tares of our appetites which often so darken and choke our minds as not to let them flower or produce those splendid fruits which alone we should wish to see born in the human heart. Thus in this way justice and self-respect, which you say Jove sent on earth to all men, are natural in each one of us. But just as however robust it is a man's body may fail when seeking to accomplish some task, so, although the potentiality for these virtues is rooted within our souls, it often fails to develop unless helped by education. For if it is to pass to actuality and to its full realization, it cannot, as I said, rely on Nature alone but needs the assistance of skilful practice and reason to purify and enlighten the soul by removing from it the dark veil of ignorance, which is the cause of most human errors, since if good and evil were easily recognized and understood everyone would always choose good and eschew evil. Thus virtue may be defined more or less as prudence and the knowledge of how to choose what is good, and vice as a kind of imprudence and ignorance, which leads us into making false judgements. This is because men never choose evil deliberately but are deceived by a certain semblance of good.'

Then signor Gaspare replied: 'Yet there are many who fully understand that they are doing evil, and still do it; and this is because, like thieves and murderers, they are more conscious of the pleasures of the moment than of the punishment they fear in the future.'

Signor Ottaviano remarked: 'True pleasure is always good, and true suffering always evil; therefore these men deceive themselves when they take false pleasures for true and true suffering for false. And so their false pleasures often earn them genuine pain. It follows that the art that teaches us to distinguish the true from the false can certainly be learned; and the virtue which enables us to choose what is genuinely good and not what wrongly appears to be so may be called true knowledge, which is more advantageous in life than any other kind, because it rids us of the ignorance which, as I said, is the cause of all the evils there are.'

At this, Pietro Bembo said: 'I do not understand, signor Ottaviano, why signor Gaspare should have to concede that all evils spring from ignorance and that there are few who realize what they are doing when they sin and do not at all deceive themselves regarding true pleasure or suffering. It is certain that even men who are incontinent form their judgement reasonably and logically, and are fully aware of the evil and sinful nature of what they desire. So they use their reason to oppose and resist their desires, and this causes the battle of pleasure and pain against judgement. Then eventually the desires prove too strong for reason, which abandons the struggle, like a ship which for a time resists the storm but finally, battered by the overwhelming fury of the winds, with anchor and rigging smashed, lets herself be driven by the tempest, unresponsive either to helm or compass. So the incontinent commit their follies with a certain hesitant remorse, as if despite themselves. And this they would not do if they did not know that what they were doing was evil; on the contrary, without any resistance from reason they would abandon themselves utterly to their desires, and in this case would not be incontinent but simply intemperate. And this is far worse, since reason plays a part in incontinence, which is therefore a less serious vice; just as continence is an imperfect virtue, since it is influenced by the emotions. In consequence, it seems to me that one cannot ascribe the follies of the incontinent to ignorance or say that they are merely deceiving themselves without sinning, when they know full well what they are doing.'

'Well,' answered signor Ottaviano, 'your argument sounds very fine. Nevertheless, I don't think that it is really valid. For although the incontinent sin in that hesitant manner, and their reason does struggle with their desires, and they realize what evil is, yet they lack full knowledge and do not understand evil as well as they need to. Possessing only a vague notion rather than any certain knowledge of evil, they allow their reason to be overcome by emotion. But if they enjoyed true knowledge there is no doubt that they would not fall into error. For reason is always overcome by desire because of ignorance, and true knowledge can never be defeated by the emotions, which originate in the body rather than the soul. And if the emotions are properly governed and controlled by reason, then they become virtuous, and if otherwise, then vicious. However, reason is so potent that it always makes the senses obey it, insinuating itself by marvellous ways and means, provided what it ought to possess is not seized by ignorance. In this manner, though a man's faculties, nerves and bones do not possess reason, when the mind begins to stir within us it is as if thought were shaking the bridle and spurring our faculties on, so that all the parts of the body prepare themselves: the feet to run, the hands to grasp or to do what the mind suggests. This is shown by what often happens when someone unknowingly eats food that tastes delicious but is really foul and disgusting; for when he finds out what it was, his mind is revolted and dismayed, and then the body responds so quickly to his judgement that he has to vomit.'

Signor Ottaviano was going on to say more, but he was then interrupted by the Magnifico Giuliano who remarked:

'If I have heard aright, you said that continence is not a perfect virtue because it is influenced by the emotions. Yet it seems to me that when there is conflict in our minds between reason and desire, the virtue which fights and gives the victory to reason ought to be considered more perfect than that which conquers when no lust or emotion opposes it. For in the latter case the person concerned does not refrain from evil out of virtue but because he has no wish to do it.'

Then signor Ottaviano said: 'Who would you think the more admirable: a commander who runs the risk of open confrontation with the enemy, and yet conquers him, or one who uses his skill and knowledge to sap the enemy's strength and render him powerless and so conquers without risk or bloodshed?'

The Magnifico replied: 'The one who conquers by less dangerous means is certainly the more praiseworthy, provided that his inevitable victory is not brought about by the enemy's ineptitude.'

'You have judged aright,' said signor Ottaviano. 'And so I tell you that continence can be compared to a commander who fights manfully and who, when the enemy is strong and powerful, conquers all the same, though not without great difficulty and risk. But unruffled temperance is like the commander who conquers and rules without opposition; and when it has not only subdued but totally extinguished the fires of lust in the mind which possesses it, like a good ruler in time of civil war, temperance destroys all seditious enemies within and hands over to reason the sceptre of absolute power. Thus this virtue does no violence to the soul, but gently infuses it with a powerful persuasion that turns it to honest ways, renders it calm and full of repose, in all things even and well-tempered, and informed in all respects with a certain harmony that adorns it with serene and unshakeable tranquillity; and so in all things it is ready to respond completely to reason and to follow wherever reason may lead with the utmost docility, like a young lamb that runs and walks alongside its mother, stops when she does, and moves only in response to her. This virtue of temperance, therefore, is wholly perfect and especially appropriate for men who rule, for it gives rise to many other virtues.'

Then Cesare Gonzaga remarked: 'Well, I don't know what virtues appropriate for a ruler can spring from temperance, if temperance, as you say, removes all the emotions from one's mind. This might be fitting in a hermit or a monk; but I can hardly think that it is becoming for a prince, who is magnanimous, liberal and valiant in arms, whatever the provocation, never to display anger or hatred or indeed kindliness or scorn or lust or any emotion at all. For how could he otherwise exert any authority either over his people or his troops?'

Signor Ottaviano replied: 'I did not say that temperance completely removes and uproots the emotions from a man's soul, nor would it be well for it to do so, since there are good elements even in the emotions. But what it does do is to make what is perverse and opposed to right conduct in the emotions responsive to reason. So it is not right, in order to remove conflicts, to extirpate the emotions altogether; for this would be like trying to suppress drunkenness by legislating against the use of wine, or forbidding anyone to run since when they do so men sometimes fall over. You are well aware that when someone is breaking in a horse he does not stop it from running or jumping but ensures that it does so at the right time and at the command of the rider. So when they are moderated by temperance the emotions are conducive to virtue, just as wrath strengthens fortitude, hatred against wicked men strengthens justice, and the other emotions strengthen other kinds of virtue. And if they were killed altogether, this would leave the reason weak and languid, so that it would be ineffectual, like the captain of a ship that is becalmed after the winds have dropped. So do not be so surprised, Cesare, if I said that temperance is the cause of many other virtues; for when a man's soul is attuned to this harmony, reason makes it readily receptive to true fortitude, which in turn makes it intrepid and unassailable, and immune to human suffering. And this is just as true of justice, the pure friend of modesty and goodness, and the queen of all the virtues, because justice teaches us to do what should be done and to eschew what is wrong. Thus justice is wholly perfect, since the other virtues perform their work through her, and she benefits both the just man and others as well. And without justice, as it is said, Jove himself could not govern his kingdom well. These virtues are also followed by magnanimity, which enhances them all, though it cannot exist alone since anyone lacking other virtues cannot be magnanimous. And then for their guide, the virtues have prudence, which consists in a certain quality of judgement in making the right decisions. The other links in this happy chain of virtues are liberality, munificence, the desire for honour, gentleness, charm, affability and many other qualities there is not the time to name. But if our courtier behaves as we have suggested he will discover these flourishing in the soul of his prince, and every day will see blossoming there more delightful flowers and fruits than there are in all the lovely gardens on earth. He himself will know great contentment, when he reminds himself that he gave his prince not what fools give, namely, gifts such as gold and silver, vases and garments (of which the prince has too many already and the giver only too few) but what is doubtless the greatest and rarest of all human virtues: the manner and method of good government. This alone would be enough to make men happy and restore to earth the golden age which is said to have existed once, when Saturn ruled.'

[. . .]

Then signor Gaspare said: 'I remember that when these gentlemen were discussing the accomplishments of the courtier they wished him to be in love. However, when we sum up what has been said so far we could come to the conclusion that the courtier who must introduce the prince to virtue through his own merits and authority must of necessity be an elderly man, for only rarely does wisdom not wait upon age, and especially as regards what we learn from experience. So I do not see how if he is advanced in years it is fitting for the courtier to be in love, seeing that, as has already been said this evening, in old men love is futile and what women take for agreeable courtesies, pleasantries and elegance in the young are in the old inept and ridiculous follies which will cause some women to detest and everyone to deride whoever indulges in them. So if this Aristotle of yours, as an elderly courtier, were to be in love and to do the things that young lovers do (like some we have seen in our own times) I fear he would forget to instruct his prince and doubtless the children would make fun of him behind his back and the ladies would hardly derive any pleasure from him other than to mock him.'

Then signor Ottaviano answered: 'As all the other qualities attributed to the courtier are suitable to him, even when he is old, I don't think it right to deprive him of the happiness of being in love.'

'On the contrary,' retorted signor Gaspare, 'to deprive him of it adds another perfection to him and enables him to live happily, free of all calamity and misery.'

Then Pietro Bembo added: 'Do you not remember, signor Gaspare, that although he is untutored in love in the game he suggested the other evening signor Ottaviano evidently knew that there are some lovers who regard as pleasurable all the storms of indignation, the outbursts of temper, the wars and the torments that they experience with their ladies? And he asked to be taught the cause of this pleasure. Therefore if our courtier were to be inflamed with the kind of love that is agreeable and without bitterness, even if elderly he would not experience any misery or suffering. And then again as a wise man, which we suppose him to be, he would not deceive himself in thinking that everything suitable for a young man to do was likewise suitable in his case. If in love, he would doubtless love in a way that would not only bring him no blame but earn him great praise and complete happiness, free of all vexation, which rarely if ever happens with younger men. And so he would not neglect to instruct his prince nor would he do anything to cause children to make fun of him.'

Then the Duchess remarked: 'I am glad, Pietro, that you have had to make little effort in our discussion this evening, because now we can have all the more confidence in giving you the task of speaking, and of teaching us about this kind of love which is so felicitous that it brings with it neither blame nor displeasure; for doubtless it would be one of the most useful and important of the endowments yet attributed to the courtier. So please, I beg you, tell us all you know about it.'

Pietro smiled and replied: 'Madam, I wouldn't wish my having said that it is permissible for old men to love to cause these ladies to suppose that I am old myself. So please give this task to someone else.'

The Duchess replied: 'You should not run away from

being reputed old in wisdom, even if you are young in years. So please go on, and don't make any more excuses.'

Then Pietro Bembo answered: 'Truly, madam, if I do have to talk on this subject I shall have to go for advice to my Lavinello's friend, the hermit.

At this, as if annoyed, signora Emilia exclaimed:

'Pietro, no one among us is more disobedient than you. So it would be only right if the Duchess were to punish you.'

Pietro, who was still smiling, answered:

'Don't be annoyed with me, madam, for pity's sake. For I shall tell you what you want.'

'Then please do so,' replied signora Emilia.

Thereupon, Pietro Bembo remained quiet for a little while. Then, having composed himself for a moment as if to speak of important things, he began as follows:

'Gentlemen, to show that old men can love not only blamelessly but sometimes more happily than the young, it will be necessary for me to enter upon a little discourse in order to make it clear what love is and what is the nature of the happiness that lovers experience. So I beg you to listen attentively, because I hope to make you realize that there is no man to whom it is unbecoming to be in love, even though he should be fifteen or twenty years older than signor Morello.'

After there was some laughter at this, Pietro Bembo continued:

'I say, therefore, that as defined by the philosophers of the ancient world Love is simply a certain longing to possess beauty; and since this longing can only be for things that are known already, knowledge must always of necessity precede desire, which by its nature wishes for what is good, but of itself is blind and so cannot perceive what is good. So Nature has ruled that every appetitive faculty, or desire, be accompanied by a cognitive faculty or power of understanding. Now in the human soul there are three faculties by which we understand or perceive things: namely, the senses, rational thought and intellect. Thus the senses desire things through sensual appetite or the kind of appetite which we share with the animals; reason desires things through rational choice, which is, strictly speaking, proper to man; and intellect, which links man to the angels, desires things through pure will. It follows that the sensual appetite desires only those things that are perceptible by the senses, whereas man's will finds its satisfaction in the contemplation of spiritual things that can be apprehended by intellect. And then man, who is rational by his very nature and is placed between the two extremes of brute matter and pure spirit, can choose to follow the senses or to aspire to the intellect, and so can direct his appetites or desires now in the one direction, now in the other. In either of these two ways, therefore, he can long for beauty, which is the quality possessed by all natural or artificial things that are composed in the good proportion and due measure that befit their nature.

'However, I shall speak of the kind of beauty I now have in mind, which is that seen in the human body and especially the face and which prompts the ardent desire we call love; and we shall argue that this beauty is an influx of the divine goodness which, like the light of the sun, is shed over all created things but especially displays itself in all its beauty when it discovers and informs a countenance which is well proportioned and composed of a certain joyous harmony of various colours enhanced by light and shadow and by symmetry and clear definition. This goodness adorns and illumines with wonderful splendour and grace the object in which it shines, like a sunbeam striking a lovely vase of polished gold set with precious gems. And thus it attracts to itself the gaze of others, and entering through their eyes it impresses itself upon the human soul, which it stirs and delights with its charm, inflaming it with passion and desire. Thus the mind is seized by desire for the beauty which it recognizes as good, and, if it allows itself to be guided by what its senses tell it, it falls into the gravest errors and judges that the body is the chief cause of the beauty which it enshrines, and so to enjoy that beauty it must necessarily achieve with it as intimate a union as possible. But this is untrue; and anyone who thinks to enjoy that beauty by possessing the body is deceiving himself and is moved not by true knowledge, arrived at by rational choice, but by a false opinion derived from the desire of the senses. So the pleasure that follows is also necessarily false and deceptive. Consequently, all those lovers who satisfy their impure desires with the women they love meet with one of two evils: either as soon as they achieve the end they desire they experience satiety and distaste and even begin to hate what they love, as if their desire repented of its error and recognized the way it had been deceived by the false judgement of the senses, which had made it believe that evil was good; or else they are still troubled by the same avidity and desire, since they have not in fact attained the end they were seeking. Admittedly, confused by their short-sighted view of things, they imagine that they are experiencing pleasure, just as sometimes a sick man dreams that he is drinking from a clear fountain. Nevertheless, they enjoy neither rest nor satisfaction, and these are precisely what they would enjoy as the natural consequences of desiring and then possessing what is good. On the contrary, deceived by the resemblance they see, they soon experience unbridled desire once more and in the same agitation as before they again find themselves with a raging and unquenchable thirst for what they hope to possess utterly. Lovers of this kind, therefore, are always most unhappy; for either they never attain their desires, and this causes them great misery, or if they do attain them they find themselves in terrible distress, and their wretchedness is even greater. For both at the beginning and during the course of this love of theirs they never know other than anguish, torment, sorrow, exertion and distress; and so lovers, it is supposed, must always be characterized by paleness and dejection, continuous sighings and weepings, mournfulness and lamentations, silences and the desire for death.

'We see, therefore, that the senses are the chief cause of this desolation of the spirit; and they are at their full strength in youth, when they are stimulated by the urges of the flesh which sap a man's powers of reason in exact proportion to their own vigour and so easily persuade the soul to yield to desire. For since it is sunk in an earthly prison and deprived of spiritual contemplation, the soul cannot of itself clearly perceive the truth when it is carrying out its duties of governing the body. So in order to understand things properly it must appeal to the senses for its first notions. In consequence it believes whatever they tell it and respects and trusts them, especially when they are so vigorous that they almost compel it; and because the senses are deceptive they fill the soul with errors and mistaken ideas. As a result, young men are invariably absorbed by this sensual kind of love and wholly rebellious against reason, and so they make themselves unworthy of enjoying the blessings and advantages that love gives to its true devotees; and the only pleasures they experience in love are the same as those enjoyed by unreasoning animals, though the distress they suffer is far more terrible than theirs. Therefore on this premise, which I insist is the absolute truth, I argue that lovers who are more mature in age experience the contrary; for in their case the soul is no longer so weighed down by the body and their natural ardour has begun to cool, and so if they are inflamed by beauty and their desire for it is guided by rational choice, they are not deceived and they possess completely the beauty they love. Consequently its possession brings them nothing but good, since beauty is goodness and so the true love of beauty is good and holy and always benefits those in whose souls the bridle of reason restrains the iniquity of the senses; and this is something the old can do far more easily than the young.

★

'So it is not unreasonable to argue also that the old can love blamelessly and more happily than the young, accepting that by old we do not mean those who are senile or whose bodily organs have grown so feeble that the soul cannot perform its operations through them, but men whose intellectual powers are still in their prime. I must also add this: namely, that in my opinion although sensual love is bad at every age, yet in the young it may be excused and perhaps in some sense even permitted. For although it brings them afflictions, dangers, exertions and all the unhappiness we have mentioned, yet there are many who perform worthy acts in order to win the favour of the women whom they love, and though these acts are not directed to a good end they are good in themselves. And so from all that bitterness they extract a little sweetness, and the adversities they endure finally teach them the error of their ways. So just as I think those young people who subdue their desires and love in a rational manner are truly heroic, I excuse those who allow themselves to be overcome by the sensual love to which human weakness inclines them, provided that they then display gentleness, courtesy, worthiness and all the other qualities these gentlemen mentioned, and that when they are no longer young they abandon it completely and leave sensual desire behind them, as the lowest rung of the ladder by which we can ascend to true love. But no blame is too severe for those who when they are old still allow the fires of passion to burn in their cold hearts and make strong reason obey their feeble senses; for they deserve the endless shame of being numbered like idiots among the animals which lack reason, because the thoughts and ways of sensual love are wholly unbecoming to men of mature years.'

Bembo then paused for a moment, as if to rest; and as everyone remained silent, signor Morello da Ortona said:

'But if there were to be found an old man more able-bodied, more vigorous and more handsome than many youths, why would you not wish that he should be allowed to love in their way?'

The Duchess laughed at this and remarked:

'If love is such an unhappy experience for the young, why, signor Morello, do you want old men as well to suffer the same unhappiness? But if you were old, as these gentlemen say, you would not plot such evil against old men.'

Signor Morello replied: 'It seems to me that the one who is plotting evil against old men is Pietro Bembo, because he wishes them to love in a way that I, for one, cannot understand. And I also think that to possess the beauty he praises so much without the body is a fantasy.'

'Do you believe, signor Morello,' asked Count Lodovico, 'that beauty is always as good as Pietro Bembo says?'

'I certainly do not,' answered signor Morello. 'On the contrary, I remember having seen many beautiful women who were evil, cruel and spiteful; and this seems to me to be nearly always the case, since beauty makes them proud, and pride makes them cruel.'

Count Lodovico replied with a smile: 'Doubtless they seem cruel to you because they do not grant you what you want. But let Pietro Bembo teach you how old men ought to desire beauty, and what they should seek from women, and with what they ought to be satisfied; and provided you keep within these limits you will discover that they are neither proud nor cruel, and they will also grant you what you want.'

Signor Morello showed his irritation at this, and he retorted:

'I don't want to learn what doesn't concern me. Let someone teach you the way in which this beauty ought to be desired by young men who are not so able-bodied or vigorous as the old.'

Then Federico, in order to calm signor Morello and to change the subject, interrupted before Count Lodovico could reply and said:

'Perhaps signor Morello is not altogether wrong in saying that beauty is not always good, for often woman's beauty causes the world endless evil, enmity, war, death and destruction, as was shown very clearly, for example, by the downfall of Troy. And for the most part beautiful women are either proud and cruel or else, as has been said, unchaste; though this last signor Morello would not consider a fault. There are also many wicked men who are endowed with good looks, and it seems that Nature has made them so in order that they may be better able to deceive, and that their agreeable appearance is the bait concealing the hook.'

Then Pietro Bembo stated: 'Do not believe that beauty is not always good.'

Here, in order to return to the original subject, Count Lodovico broke in and remarked:

'Since signor Morello is not interested in learning what concerns him so deeply, teach it to me, and show me how old men may win the happiness of love; for I shall not worry if I cause myself to be considered old, provided I profit by it.'

Pietro Bembo said with a smile: 'First I wish to correct the error made by these gentlemen, and then I shall satisfy you as well.'

Then he continued as follows:

'Gentlemen, beauty is a sacred thing, and I should not wish any of us to act like profane and sacrilegious men in speaking ill of it and thereby incurring the wrath of God. So as a warning for signor Morello and Federico, lest they are punished in the way most suitable for those who despise beauty, and lose their sight like Stesichorus, I say that beauty springs from God and is like a circle, the centre of which is goodness. And so just as one cannot have a circle without a centre, so one cannot have beauty without goodness. In consequence, only rarely does an evil soul dwell in a beautiful body, and so outward beauty is a true sign of inner goodness. This loveliness, indeed, is impressed upon the body in varying degrees as a token by which the soul can be recognized for what it is, just as with trees the beauty of the blossom testifies to the goodness of the fruit. The same is true of the human body, as we know from the way physiognom-ists often establish a man's character and sometimes even his thoughts from his countenance. Moreover, even in animals the qualities of the soul as far as possible impress themselves upon the body and can be perceived from their physical appearance. Consider how clearly we can perceive anger, ferocity and pride in the face of the lion, the horse and the eagle; and a pure and simple innocence in lambs and doves; evil guile in foxes and wolves, and so with nearly all the animals.

'Therefore for the most part the ugly are also evil, and the beautiful good. And it can be said that beauty is the pleasant, gay, charming and desirable face of the good, and that ugliness is the dark, disagreeable, unpleasant and sorry face of evil. And no matter what things you study, you will always find that those which are good and useful are also graced with beauty. Consider the structure of this great fabric of the universe, which was created by God for the health and preservation of all His creatures. The bowl of heaven, adorned with so many celestial lamps, and the earth in the centre, surrounded by the elements and sustained by its own weight; the sun, illuminating all things as it revolves, in winter approaching the lowest sign, and then by degrees ascending to the other side; the moon, which derives its light from the sun, in accord with whether the sun is approaching or drawing away; and the five other stars which separately travel the same course: these all influence each other so profoundly through the coherence of the natural order that if they changed in the slightest they could no longer exist together and the universe would crumble. Moreover, they have such beauty and loveliness that the human mind cannot conceive anything more graceful. Consider next the structure of man, who may be called a little universe in himself. We see that every part of his body is in the natural order of things made by design and not by chance and that his form as a whole is so beautiful that it is difficult to decide whether it is utility or grace that is given more to the human face and body by its various parts, such as the eyes, nose, mouth, ears, arms and breast. The same can be said of all the animals. Consider the feathers of birds and the leaves and branches of trees, which are given by Nature to preserve their being, and yet which are also of the greatest loveliness. Now let us leave Nature and come to human art. What is so necessary for a ship as the prow, the sides, the mainyards, the mast, the sails, the helm, the oars, the anchor and the rigging? Yet all these things are so attractive that anyone looking at them must conclude they exist as much for pleasure as for use. Columns and architraves support lofty galleries and palaces, but they are no less pleasing to the eye than they are useful to the building. When men first began to build they included the middle ridge in their churches and houses not to embellish their buildings but to allow the water to flow off without trouble on either side; nevertheless, attractiveness of appearance soon became as important as usefulness, so that if a church were to be built in a land which never knew rain or hail, it would seem to lack both dignity and beauty if left without the ridge of a roof.

'Thus to call anything beautiful, even the world itself, constitutes the highest praise. It is praised when we say such things as: beautiful sky, beautiful earth, beautiful sea, beautiful rivers, beautiful countryside, beautiful woods, trees and gardens; or beautiful cities, churches, houses and armies. In short, this gracious and sacred beauty is the supreme adornment of everything; and it can be said that in some manner the good and the beautiful are identical, especially in the human body. And the proximate cause of physical beauty is, in my opinion, the beauty of the soul which since it shares in true supernatural beauty makes whatever it touches resplendent and lovely, especially if the body it inhabits is not of such base material that the soul cannot impress on it its own quality. Therefore beauty is the true trophy of the soul's victory, when with her heavenly power she rules over material nature and with her light dispels the darkness of the body. We must not say, therefore, that beauty makes women proud or cruel, though this may seem to be the case to signor Morello; neither should we impute to beautiful women those enmities, deaths and destructions which are caused by the unrestrained desires of men. To be sure, I shall not deny that we can also find in the world beautiful women who are unchaste. But it is all the same not their beauty which makes them so; on the contrary, because of the bond between beauty and goodness, their beauty turns them away from impurity and leads them to the path of virtuous conduct. But sometimes evil training, the continual urgings of their lovers, gifts, poverty, hope, deceits, fear and a thousand other causes can defeat the steadfastness even of good and beautiful women; and for this and other reasons handsome men can also become wicked.'

Then Cesare remarked: 'If what signor Gaspare alleged yesterday is true, then there is no doubt that women who are beautiful are more chaste than those who are ugly.'

'And what did I allege?' asked signor Gaspare.

'If I remember correctly,' replied Cesare, 'you said that women who are wooed always refuse to satisfy their suitor, and that those who are not, do the wooing themselves. And it is certain that the beautiful are always more wooed and pursued in love than the ugly; therefore the beautiful always refuse, and so they are more chaste than those ugly women who, as they have no suitors, do the wooing themselves.'

Bembo smiled and said: 'There can be no answer to this argument.'

Then he added: 'It also often happens that, like the other senses, our sight can be deceived and can judge to be beautiful a face that is not so at all. For example some women occasionally display in their eyes and looks a certain enticing and suggestive immodesty which is called beauty by many who find these traits pleasing because they promise them the chance of gaining what they desire. But in truth this is simply meretricious impudence, and unworthy of so honoured and sacred a name.'

Pietro Bembo then fell silent, but he was urged to say more about this kind of love and about the true way in which beauty should be enjoyed; and at length he said:

'I think I have shown clearly enough that old men can be happier in love than the young; and this was my premise. So it is not for me to add any more.'

Count Lodovico replied: 'You have demonstrated the unhappiness of the young better than the happiness of the old, whom you have not yet taught what path to follow in love but merely instructed to let themselves be guided by reason. And many people consider that it is impossible to reconcile love with reason.'

Bembo was still determined to say no more, but the Duchess begged that he should do so, and therefore he continued:

'It would be too unfortunate for humanity if our soul, in which such ardent desire can so easily arise, were forced to find nourishment only in what it has in common with the animals and could not direct its desire to its nobler element. So, as this is your wish, I will not refuse to discuss this noble theme. And since I know that I am unworthy to speak of Love's sacred mysteries, I pray him so to inspire my thoughts and words that I can teach this excellent courtier of ours how to love in a manner beyond the capacity of the vulgar crowd. And because I have since boyhood dedicated my life to him, may my words now conform to this intention and redound to his credit. I maintain, then, that since in youth human nature is so inclined to the senses, while the courtier is young he may be allowed to love in a sensual manner; but if in more mature years he should be inflamed with this amorous desire, he must proceed with circumspection and take care not to deceive himself or let himself experience the distress which in young men deserves compassion rather than blame but in old men blame rather than compassion.

'Therefore when he sets eyes on some beautiful and attractive woman, with charming ways and gentle manner, and being skilled in love recognizes that his spirit responds to hers, as soon as he notices that his eyes fasten on her image and carry it to his heart and his soul begins to take pleasure in contemplating her and feels an influx that gradually arouses and warms it, and those vivacious spirits shining from her eyes constantly add fresh fuel to the fire, then he should at the very beginning procure a swift remedy and alert his reason in order to defend with its help the fortress of his heart, and so close the passes to the senses and to desire that they cannot enter either by force or deception. If the flame is extinguished, so is the danger. But if it perseveres or grows, then in the knowledge that he has been captured the courtier should determine to eschew all the ugliness of vulgar passion and guided by reason set forth on the path of divine love. Then first he must reflect that the body in which beauty shines is not the source from which it springs, and on the contrary that beauty, being incorporeal and, as we have said, a ray of the supernatural, loses much of its nobility when fused with base and corruptible matter: for the more perfect it is, the less matter it contains, and it is most perfect when completely separated from matter. He must also reflect that just as a man cannot hear with his palate or smell with his ears, beauty can in no way be enjoyed nor can the desire it arouses in our souls be satisfied through the sense of touch but solely through what has beauty for its true object, namely, the faculty of sight. So he should ignore the blind judgement of these senses and enjoy with his eyes the radiance, the grace, the loving ardour, the smiles, the mannerisms and all the other agreeable adornments of the woman he loves. Similarly, let him use his hearing to enjoy the sweetness of her voice, the modulation of her words and, if she is a musician, the music she plays. In this way, through the channels of these two faculties, which have little to do with corporeal things and are servants of reason, he will nourish his soul on the most delightful food and will not allow desire for the body to arouse in him any appetite that is at all impure. Next, with the greatest reverence the lover should honour, please and obey his lady, cherish her even more than himself, put her convenience and pleasure before his own, and love the beauty of her soul no less than that of her body. He should, therefore, be at pains to keep her from going astray and by his wise precepts and admonishments always seek to make her modest, temperate and truly chaste; and he must ensure that her thoughts are always pure and unsullied by any trace of evil. And thus, by sowing virtue in the garden of her lovely soul, he will gather the fruits of faultless behaviour and experience exquisite pleasure from their taste. And this will be the true engendering and expression of beauty in beauty, which some say is the purpose of love. In this manner, our courtier will be most pleasing to his lady, and she will always be submissive, charming and affable and as anxious to please him as she is to be loved by him; and the desires of both will be very pure and harmonious, and consequently they will be perfectly happy.'

Then signor Morello remarked: 'In reality, this engendering of beauty in beauty must mean the begetting of a beautiful child in a beautiful woman; and it would seem to me a far clearer sign that she loved her lover if she pleased him in this than if she treated him merely with the affability you mention.'

Bembo laughed and replied: 'You mustn't go beyond the bounds, signor Morello; nor indeed does a woman grant just a token of affection when she gives her lover her beauty, which is precious to her, and along the paths into her soul, namely, sight and hearing, sends the glances of her eyes, the image of her face, her voice and her words, which penetrate her lover's heart and convey the proof of her love.'

Signor Morello then said: 'Glances and words can be false witnesses, and often are. So anyone who has no better pledge of love is in my opinion most uncertain; and truly I was expecting you to make this lady of yours a little more courteous and generous towards the courtier than the Magnifico made his. However, I think both of you are acting in the same way as those judges who pronounce sentence against their own people in order to seem wise.'

'I am perfectly willing,' Bembo continued, 'for this lady to be far more courteous to my elderly courtier than signor Magnifico's lady is to the young courtier. And this is with good reason, for my courtier will wish only for seemly things, all of which she may therefore concede to him quite innocently. But the Magnifico's lady, who is not so certain of the young courtier's modesty, should concede him only what is seemly and deny him what is not. Therefore my courtier, who obtains all he asks for, is happier than the other, who is granted some of his requests but refused others. And to help you understand even better that rational love is happier than sensual love, I say that sometimes the same things should be denied in sensual love and granted in rational love, because in the former context they are unseemly, and in the latter, seemly. Thus to please her gracious lover, besides granting him pleasant smiles, intimate and secret conversations, and the liberty to joke and jest and touch hands, the lady may very reasonably and innocently go so far as to grant a kiss, which in sensual love, according to the Magnifico's rules, is not permitted. For as a kiss is a union of body and soul, there is a risk that the sensual lover may incline more to the body than the soul; but the rational lover knows that although the mouth is part of the body nevertheless it provides a channel for words, which are the interpreters of the soul, and for the human breath or spirit. Consequently, the rational lover delights when he joins his mouth to that of the lady he loves in a kiss, not in order to arouse in himself any unseemly desire but because he feels that this bond opens the way for their souls which, attracted by their mutual desire, each pour themselves into the other's body in turn and so mingle that each of them possesses two souls, and it is as if a single spirit composed of the two governs their two bodies. So the kiss may be called a spiritual rather than physical union because it exerts such power over the soul that it draws it to itself and separates it from the body. For this reason, all chaste lovers desire a kiss as a union of souls; and thus when inspired to love Plato said that in kissing the soul comes to the lips in order to leave the body. And because the separation of the soul from things that are perceptible to the senses and its complete union with spiritual things can be signified by the kiss, in his inspired book of the *Song of Songs* Solomon says: "let him kiss me with the kiss of his mouth", in order to express the wish that his soul be transported by divine love to the contemplation of celestial beauty and by its intimate union with this beauty might forsake the body.'

All were listening very attentively to what Bembo was saying; and then, after a moment's pause, he added:

'Since you have made me begin to teach the courtier who is no longer young about love that is truly happy, I want to lead him a little further still. For to stop at this point is very dangerous, because, as we have said several times already, the soul is strongly inclined towards the senses; and although reason may choose well in its operation and recognize that beauty does not arise from the body, and therefore act as a check to impure desires, yet the constant contemplation of physical beauty often perverts true judgement. And even if no other evil resulted from this, absence from the person one loves causes much suffering. This is because when beauty is physically present, its influx into the lover's soul brings him intense pleasure, and by warming his heart it arouses and melts certain hidden and congealed powers which the warmth of love nourishes and causes to flow and well up round his heart and send through his eyes those spirits or most subtle vapours, composed of the purest and brightest part of the blood, to receive the image of her beauty and embellish it with a thousand varied adornments. In consequence, the soul is filled with wonder and delight; it is frightened and yet it rejoices; as if dazed, it experiences along with its pleasure the fear and reverence invariably inspired by sacred things, and it believes it has entered into its Paradise.

'Therefore the lover who is intent only on physical beauty loses all this good and happiness as soon as the woman he loves by her absence leaves his eyes deprived of their splendour and, consequently, his soul widowed of its good. For, since her beauty is far away, there is no influx of affection to warm his heart as it did when she was there, and so the openings of his body become arid and dry; yet the memory of her beauty still stirs the powers of his soul a little, so that they seek to pour those spirits forth. Although their paths are blocked and there is no exit for them, they still strive to depart, and thus tormented and enclosed they begin to prick the soul and cause it to suffer bitterly, as children do when the teeth begin to grow through their tender gums. This causes the tears, the sighs, the anguish and the torments of lovers, because the soul is in constant pain and turmoil and almost raging in fury until its cherished beauty appears once more; and then suddenly it is calmed and breathes again, and wholly absorbed it draws strength from the delicious food before it and wishes never to part from such a ravishing vision. Therefore, to escape the torment caused by absence and to enjoy beauty without suffering, with the help of reason the courtier should turn his desire completely away from the body to beauty alone. He should contemplate beauty as far as he is able in its own simplicity and purity, create it in his imagination as an abstraction distinct from any material form, and thus make it lovely and dear to his soul, and enjoy it there always, day and night and in every time and place, without fear of ever losing it; and he will always remember that the body is something altogether distinct from beauty, whose perfection it diminishes rather than enhances. In this way the courtier of ours who is no longer young will put himself out of reach of the anguish and distress invariably experienced by the young in the form of jealousy, suspicion, disdain, anger, despair and a certain tempestuous fury that occasionally leads them so much astray that some not only beat the women they love but take their own lives. He will do no injury to the husband, father, brothers or family of the lady he loves; he will cause her no shame; he will not be forced sometimes to drag his eyes away and curb his tongue for fear of revealing his desires to others; or to endure suffering when they part or during her absence. For he will always carry the treasure that is so precious to him safe in his heart; and by the power of his imagination he will also make her beauty far more lovely than it is in reality.

'However, among all these blessings the lover will find one that is far greater still, if he will determine to make use of this love as a step by which to climb to another that is far more sublime; and this will be possible if he continually reflects how narrowly he is confined by always limiting himself to the contemplation of a single body. And so in order to escape from this confinement, he will gradually add so many adornments to his idea of beauty that, by uniting all possible forms of beauty in his mind, he will form a universal concept and so reduce all the many varieties to the unity of that single beauty which sheds itself over human nature as a whole. And thus he will come to contemplate not the particular beauty of a single woman but the universal beauty which adorns all human bodies: and then, dazzled by this greater light, he will not concern himself with the lesser; burning with a more perfect flame, he will feel little esteem for what he formerly prized so greatly. Now this stage of love, although so noble that few attain it, still cannot be called perfect. For the human imagination is a corporeal faculty and acquires knowledge only through the data supplied to it by the senses, and so it is not wholly purged of the darkness of material things. Thus although it may consider this universal beauty in the abstract and simply in itself, yet it perceives it not at all clearly nor within a certain ambiguity because of the affinities that the images it forms have with the body itself; and so those who reach this stage of love are like fledglings which on their feeble wings can lift themselves a little in flight but dare not stray far from the nest or trust themselves to the winds and the open sky.

'Therefore when our courtier has arrived at this stage, even though he can be called most happy in comparison with those lovers who are still sunk in the miseries of sensual love, I wish him not to be satisfied but to move boldly onwards along the sublime path of love and follow his guide towards the goal of true happiness. So instead of directing his thoughts to the outward world, as those must do who wish to consider bodily beauty, let him turn within himself to contemplate what he sees with the eyes of the mind, which begin to be penetrating and clear-sighted once those of the body have lost the flower of their delight; and in this manner, having shed all evil, purged by the study of true philosophy, directed towards the life of the spirit, and practised in the things of the intellect, the soul turns to contemplate its own substance, and as if awakened from deepest sleep it opens the eyes which all men possess but few use and perceives in itself a ray of that light which is the true image of the angelic beauty that has been transmitted to it, and of which in turn it transmits a faint impression to the body. Thus, when it has become blind to earthly things, the soul opens its eyes wide to those of heaven; and sometimes when the faculties of the body are totally absorbed by assiduous contemplation, or bound to sleep, no longer hindered by their influence the soul tastes a certain hidden savour of the true angelic beauty, and ravished by the loveliness of that light it begins to burn and to pursue the beauty it sees so avidly that it seems almost drunk and beside itself in its desire to unite with it. For the soul then believes that it has discovered the traces of God, in the contemplation of which it seeks its final repose and bliss. And so, consumed in this most joyous flame, it ascends to its noblest part, which is the intellect; and there, no more overshadowed by the dark night of earthly things, it glimpses the divine beauty itself. Even so, it does not yet enjoy this perfectly, since it contemplates it only in its own particular intellect, which cannot comprehend universal beauty in all its immensity. And so, not even satisfied with bestowing this blessing, love gives the soul greater happiness still. For just as from the particular beauty of a single body it guides the soul to the universal beauty of all bodies, so, in the last stage of perfection, it guides the soul from the particular intellect to the universal intellect. And from there, aflame with the sacred fire of true divine love, the soul flies to unite itself with the angelic nature, and it not only abandons the senses but no longer has need of reason itself. For, transformed into an angel, it understands all intelligible things and without any veil or cloud it gazes on the wide sea of pure divine beauty, which it receives into itself to enjoy the supreme happiness the senses cannot comprehend.

'The kinds of beauty which every day we see in corruptible bodies with these clouded eyes of ours (and which even so are only dreams and faint shadows) appear to be so lovely and graceful that they often kindle in us a most ardent fire and cause such delight that we count no happiness the equal of what we sometimes feel because of a single glance we may receive from the eyes of the woman we love, so what happy wonder, what blessed awe must we think is that which possesses the soul when it attains the vision of divine beauty! What sweet flame, what ravishing fire must we believe that to be which springs from the source of supreme and true beauty, the fountain of all other beauty which never increases or diminishes! Always beautiful; most simple of itself and equally in all its parts; like only to itself and sharing in nothing other than itself; it is yet so beautiful that all other beautiful things derive their beauty from it. And this is the beauty indistinguishable from the highest good, which by its light calls and draws all things to it and which not only gives intellect to intellectual beings, reason to rational beings and the senses and the desire for life to sensual beings, but also transmits to the very plants and rocks, as an imprint of itself, motion and the instinct of their own particular nature. This love, therefore, is as greater and happier than the others as the cause that produces it is greater. And thus, just as material fire refines gold, so this most sacred fire consumes and destroys everything that is mortal in our souls and quickens and beautifies the celestial part which previously, because of the senses, was dead and buried. This is the pyre on which the poets write that Hercules was burned on the summit of Mount Oeta and through whose fire he became divine and immortal after death; this is the burning bush of Moses, the parted tongues of fire, the fiery chariot of Elias, which doubles the grace and happiness of those souls worthy to see it, when it leaves the earth below and flies towards heaven. So let us direct all the thoughts and powers of our soul towards this most sacred light which shows us the path that leads to heaven; and following after it and divesting ourselves of the human passions in which we were clothed when we fell, let us ascend by the ladder whose lowest rung bears the image of sensual beauty to the sublime mansion where dwells the celestial, adorable and true beauty which lies hidden in the secret recesses of the Almighty where profane eyes may not see it. And here we shall find a most happy end to our desires, true rest from our labours, a sure remedy for our miseries, a wholesome

medicine for our infirmities, a most safe harbour from
the raging storms of the tempestuous sea of this life.

'O most sacred Love, what tongue is there that can praise
you worthily? Full of beauty, goodness and wisdom, you
flow from the union of beauty, goodness and divine
wisdom, there you dwell, and through it you return to
it perpetually. Graciously binding the universe together,
midway between celestial and earthly things, by your
benign disposition you direct the heavenly powers in
their government of the lower, and turning the minds
of men to their source, you unite them with it. You unite
the elements in harmony, inspire Nature to produce,
and move all that is born to the perpetuation of life. You
join together the things that are separate, give perfection
to the imperfect, likeness to the unlike, friendship to the
hostile, fruit to the earth, tranquillity to the sea, its
life-giving light to the sky. You are the father of true
pleasures, of all blessings, of peace, of gentleness and of
good will; the enemy of rough savagery and vileness;
the beginning and the end of every good. And since you
delight to inhabit the flower of beautiful bodies and
beautiful souls, and there sometimes consent to reveal a
little of yourself to those worthy to see you, I believe
that you now dwell here among us. Consent then, O
Lord, to hear our prayers, pour yourself into our hearts,
and with the radiance of your most sacred fire illumine
our darkness and like a trusted guide show us the right
path through this blind maze. Correct the falsity of our
senses, and after our long delirium give us the true
substance of goodness. Quicken our intellects with the

incense of spirituality and make us so attuned to the celestial harmony that there is no longer room within us for any discord of passion. Inebriate our souls at the inexhaustible fountain of contentment that always delights and never satiates and that gives a taste of true blessedness to whoever drinks from its living and limpid waters. With the rays of your light cleanse our eyes of their misty ignorance, so that they may no longer prize mortal beauty but know that the things which they first thought to see are not, and that those they did not see truly are. Accept the sacrifice of our souls; and burn them in the living flame that consumes all earthly dross, so that wholly freed from the body they may unite with divine beauty in a sweet and perpetual bond and that we, liberated from our own selves, like true lovers can be transformed into the object of our love and soar above the earth to join the feast of the angels, where, with ambrosia and immortal nectar for our food, we may at last die a most happy death in life, as did those ancient Fathers whose souls, by the searing power of contemplation, you ravished from their bodies to unite with God.'

Having spoken in that way with such vehemence that he seemed transported out of himself, Bembo then remained silent and still, looking towards heaven, as if dazed. And then signora Emilia, who together with all the others had listened to all he had to say with the utmost attention, plucked the hem of his robe and said:

'Take care, Pietro, that with these thoughts of yours you too do not cause your soul to leave your body.'

'Madam,' answered Pietro, 'that would not be the first miracle that love has worked in me.'

Then the Duchess and all the others began once again to insist that Bembo should continue his discourse; and everyone almost seemed to feel in his mind a spark of the divine love that had inspired Bembo himself. They were all anxious to hear more, but he then added:

'Gentlemen, I have said all that was dictated to me on the spur of the moment by the holy frenzy of love. And now that its inspiration seems to have failed, I would not know what to say; and I think that love does not wish its secrets to be revealed any further, or that the courtier should pass beyond the stage I have been graciously permitted to show him; and so perhaps I may speak no further about this subject.'

'Truly,' said the Duchess, 'if the courtier who is no longer young is such that he is able to follow the path you have shown him he should rightly be content with such great happiness and feel no envy of the young.'

Then Cesare Gonzaga remarked: 'The road that leads to happiness seems to me so steep that I hardly think anyone can travel it.'

And then signor Gaspare added: 'I think to travel this road would be difficult for men, but impossible for women.'

Signora Emilia laughed and said:

'Signor Gaspare, if you return to giving us so many insults, I promise you will not be forgiven again.'

Signor Gaspare replied: 'It is no insult to you to say that the souls of women are not as purged of the passions

as those of men or as versed in contemplation as Pietro
has said those which are to taste divine love must be.
Thus do we not read that any woman has ever received
this grace, but we do read of many men who have,
such as Plato, Socrates, Plotinus and many others; and
similarly many of our holy Fathers, such as St Francis,
upon whom an ardent messenger of love impressed the
most holy seal of the five wounds. And only the power
of love could transport the Apostle St Paul to the vision
of those secrets of which no man is allowed to speak, or
show St Stephen the heavens opening.'

Then the Magnifico Giuliano replied:

'But women would not be surpassed by men in the
slightest as far as this is concerned: for Socrates himself
confessed that all the mysteries of love that he knew had
been revealed to him by a woman, the famous Diotima,
and the angel who pierced St Francis with the fire of
love has also made several women of our own time
worthy of the same seal. You should also remember that
many sins were forgiven St Mary Magdalene because
she loved much and that she, perhaps in no less a state
of grace than St Paul, was many times rapt to the third
heaven by angelic love, and remember many others
who, as I told at greater length yesterday, for the love of
Christ's name have cared nothing for their own life,
nor have they feared tortures or any manner of death,
however horrible and cruel. And these were not old, as
Pietro wishes his courtier to be, but tender and delicate
girls, of the age at which he says sensual love should be
allowed to men.'

*

Signor Gaspare was preparing to reply; but then the Duchess said:

'Let Pietro Bembo be the judge of this, and let us abide by his decision as to whether or not women are as capable of divine love as men. But, as the argument between you could last too long, it would be as well to postpone it until tomorrow.'

'Rather, till this evening,' said Cesare Gonzaga.

'Why this evening?' asked the Duchess.

Cesare replied: 'Because it is already day'; and he showed her the light that was beginning to come in through the clefts of the windows. Then they all rose to their feet, greatly astonished, because it did not seem that the discussion had lasted longer than usual, but as they had started far later and taken greater pleasure in it, those gentlemen had been so absorbed that they had not noticed the way time was passing; nor did anyone feel at all tired: and this often happens when the accustomed time of sleep is spent in wakefulness. So when the windows on the side of the palace that faces the lofty peak of Mount Catria had been opened, they saw that dawn had already come to the east, with the beauty and colour of a rose, and all the stars had been scattered, save only the lovely mistress of heaven, Venus, who guards the confines of night and day. From there, there seemed to come a delicate breeze, filling the air with biting cold, and among the murmuring woods on nearby hills wakening the birds into joyous song. Then all, having taken their respectful leave of the Duchess, went to their rooms, without torches, for the light of day was sufficient; and, as they were about to leave the room, the Prefect turned to the Duchess and said:

'Madam, to settle the argument between signor Gaspare and the Magnifico, we shall come with our judge this evening earlier than we did yesterday.'

Signora Emilia replied: 'On condition that if signor Gaspare should want to criticize women and slander them in his usual manner he shall give his bond to stand trial, for I arraign him as a fugitive from justice.'